COLLECTIONS
FOR YOUNG SCHOLARS™

VOLUME 2   BOOK 1

Being Brave

Rich and Poor

Fossils

Kindness

Art by Loretta Krupinski

COLLECTIONS FOR YOUNG SCHOLARS™

VOLUME 2 BOOK I

PROGRAM AUTHORS
Carl Bereiter
Ann Brown
Marlene Scardamalia
Valerie Anderson
Joe Campione

CONSULTING AUTHORS
Michael Pressley
Iva Carruthers
Bill Pinkney

OPEN COURT PUBLISHING COMPANY
CHICAGO AND PERU, ILLINOIS

CHAIRMAN
M. Blouke Carus

PRESIDENT
André W. Carus

EDUCATION DIRECTOR
Carl Bereiter

CONCEPT
Barbara Conteh

EXECUTIVE EDITOR
Shirley Graudin

MANAGING EDITOR
Sheelagh McGurn

SENIOR PROJECT EDITOR
Nancy Johnson

PROJECT EDITOR
Ana Tiesman

ART DIRECTOR
John Grandits

VICE-PRESIDENT, PRODUCTION
AND MANUFACTURING
Chris Vancalbergh

PERMISSIONS COORDINATOR
Diane Sikora

COVER ARTIST
Loretta Krupinski

Printed in the United States of America

ISBN 0-8126-2148-4

15 14 13 12 11

4

ACKNOWLEDGMENTS

Grateful acknowledgment is given to the following publishers and copyright owners for permission granted to reprint selections from their publications. All possible care has been taken to trace ownership and secure permission for each selection included.

Atheneum Publishers, an imprint of Macmillan Publishing Co.: "Fossils" from *Something New Begins* by Lilian Moore, copyright © 1982 by Lilian Moore.

Curtis Brown, Ltd., and the Estate of Jack Kent: *The Simple Prince* by Jane Yolen, illustrated by Jack Kent, text copyright © 1978 by Jane Yolen, illustrations copyright © 1978 by Jack Kent.

Barbara Bruno: "Monster Tracks," text and illustrations by Barbara Bruno from the February 1991 issue of *Cricket* magazine, copyright © 1991 by Barbara Bruno.

Childrens Press, Inc., Chicago: *Sally Ride, Astronaut: An American First* by June Behrens, text copyright © 1984 by Childrens Press, Inc.

Creative Education, Inc.: *Clara Barton: Red Cross Pioneer* by Matthew G. Grant, text copyright © 1974 by Creative Education, Inc.

Flammarion: *Cinderella* by Charles Perrault, copyright © 1977 by Flammarion.

Greenwillow Books, a division of William Morrow & Co., Inc.: "Iguanodon" and "Seismosaurus" from *Tyrannosaurus Was a Beast* by Jack Prelutsky, text copyright © 1988 by Jack Prelutsky. *Music, Music for Everyone* by Vera B. Williams, copyright © 1984 by Vera B. Williams.

Harcourt Brace & Co.: Illustration for "Fossils" from *Dinosaurs*, edited by Lee Bennett Hopkins, illustrated by Murray Tinkelman, illustration copyright © 1987 by Murray Tinkelman.

HarperCollins Publishers: "Dragons and Giants" from *Frog and Toad Together* by Arnold Lobel, copyright © 1971, 1972 by Arnold Lobel. *Fossils Tell of Long Ago* by Aliki, copyright © 1972, 1990 by Aliki Brandenberg.

Henry Holt and Co., Inc.: *The Empty Pot*, written and illustrated by Demi, copyright © 1990 by Demi.

Little, Brown and Co. and Walker Books Limited: "The North Wind and the Sun" from *The Best of Aesop's Fables*, retold by Margaret Clark, illustrated by Charlotte Voake, text copyright © 1990 by Margaret Clark, illustrations copyright © 1990 by Charlotte Voake.

Macmillan Publishing Co., a division of Macmillan, Inc.: *Mushroom in the Rain* by Mirra Ginsburg, illustrated by Jose Aruego and Ariane Dewey, text copyright © 1974 by Mirra Ginsburg, illustrations copyright © 1974 by Jose Aruego and Ariane Dewey.

G. P. Putnam's Sons: *The Legend of the Bluebonnet*, retold and illustrated by Tomie dePaola, copyright © 1983 by Tomie dePaola.

Random House, Inc.: *Molly the Brave and Me* by Jane O'Connor, illustrated by Sheila Hamanaka, text copyright © 1990 by Jane O'Connor, illustrations copyright © 1990 by Sheila Hamanaka.

Linda Robbins: "Amadou's Story" by Linda Robbins, copyright © 1990 by Linda Robbins.

Scholastic Inc., New York: *The Hole in the Dike*, retold by Norma Green, illustrated by Eric Carle, text copyright © 1974 by Norma Green, illustrations copyright © 1974 by Eric Carle. *The Elves and the Shoemaker*, retold by Freya Littledale, illustrated by Brinton Turkle, copyright © 1975 by Freya Littledale and Brinton Turkle.

Viking Penguin, a division of Penguin Books USA Inc.: *The Dinosaur Who Lived in My Backyard* by B. G. Hennessy, illustrated by Susan Davis, text copyright © 1988 B. G. Hennessy, illustrations copyright © 1988 by Susan Davis. *Corduroy* by Don Freeman, copyright © 1968 by Don Freeman.

Photography
19 Van Williams
49 Jon Gilbert Fox
83 Peter Ziebel

5

BEING BRAVE

7 🕸

RICH AND POOR

FOSSILS

11 ❧

KINDNESS

BEING BRAVE

DRAGONS AND GIANTS
written and illustrated by Arnold Lobel

F rog and Toad were reading a book together.

"The people in this book are brave," said Toad.

"They fight dragons and giants, and they are never afraid."

"I wonder if we are brave," said Frog.

Frog and Toad looked into a mirror.

"We look brave," said Frog.

"Yes, but are we?" asked Toad.

Frog and Toad went outside.

"We can try to climb this mountain," said Frog. "That should tell us if we are brave."

Frog went leaping over rocks, and Toad came puffing up behind him.

They came to a dark cave. A big snake came out of the cave.

"Hello lunch," said the snake when he saw Frog and Toad. He opened his wide mouth. Frog and Toad jumped away. Toad was shaking.

"I am not afraid!" he cried.

They climbed higher, and they heard a loud noise. Many large stones were rolling down the mountain.

"It's an avalanche!" cried Toad.

Frog and Toad jumped away.

Frog was trembling.

"I am not afraid!" he shouted.

They came to the top of the mountain. The shadow of a hawk fell over them. Frog and Toad jumped under a rock. The hawk flew away.

"We are not afraid!" screamed Frog and Toad at the same time. Then they ran down the mountain very fast. They ran past the place where they saw the avalanche. They ran past the place where they saw the snake. They ran all the way to Toad's house.

"Frog, I am glad to have a brave friend like you," said Toad. He jumped into the bed and pulled the covers over his head.

"And I am happy to know a brave person like you, Toad," said Frog. He jumped into the closet and shut the door.

Toad stayed in the bed, and Frog stayed in the closet.

They stayed there for a long time, just feeling very brave together.

MEET ARNOLD LOBEL, AUTHOR AND ILLUSTRATOR

During summer vacations, Arnold Lobel and his family spent time in Vermont. His children caught many frogs and toads. Sometimes they took them home to New York to keep as pets for the year. The following summer, they would return the creatures where they had found them. Arnold Lobel said, "I loved those little creatures and I think they led to the creation of my two most famous characters, Frog and Toad."

THE HOLE IN THE DIKE

retold by Norma Green
illustrated by Eric Carle

A long time ago, a boy named Peter lived in
Holland. He lived with his mother and father
in a cottage next to a tulip field.
Peter loved to look at the old windmills turning slowly.

He loved to look at the sea. In Holland, the land is very low, and the sea is very high. The land is kept safe and dry by high, strong walls called dikes.

Peter wheeled his bike to the road on top of the dike. It had rained for several days, and the water looked higher than usual.

Peter thought, "It's lucky that the dikes are high and strong. Without these dikes, the land would be flooded and everything would be washed away."

Suddenly he heard a soft, gurgling noise. He saw a small stream of water trickling through a hole in the dike below.

Peter got off his bike to see what was wrong.

He couldn't believe his eyes. There in the big strong dike was a leak!

Peter slid down to the bottom of the dike. He put his finger in the hole to keep the water from coming through.

He looked around for help, but he could not see anyone on the road. He shouted. Maybe someone in the nearby field would hear him, he thought.

23 🐢

Only his echo answered. Everyone had gone home.

Peter knew that if he let the water leak through the hole in the dike, the hole would get bigger and bigger. Then the sea would come gushing through. The fields and the houses and the windmills would all be flooded.

Peter looked around for something to plug up the leak so he could go to the village for help.

He put a stone in the hole, then a stick. But the stone and the stick were washed away by the water.

Peter had to stay there alone. He had to use all his strength to keep the water out.

From time to time he called for help. But no one heard him.

All night long Peter kept his finger in the dike.

His fingers grew cold and numb. He wanted to sleep, but he couldn't give up.

    At last, early in the morning, Peter heard a welcome
sound. Someone was coming! It was the milk cart
rumbling down the road.

    Peter shouted for help. The milkman was surprised to
hear someone near that road so early in the morning.
He stopped and looked around.

"Help!!" Peter shouted. "Here I am, at the bottom of the dike. There's a leak in the dike. Help! Help!"

The man saw Peter and hurried down to him. Peter showed him the leak and the little stream of water coming through.

Peter asked the milkman to hurry to the village. "Tell the people. Ask them to send some men to repair the dike right away!"

The milkman went as fast as he could. Peter had to stay with his finger in the dike.

At last the men from the village came. They set to
work to repair the leak.

All the people thanked Peter. They carried him on their shoulders, shouting, "Make way for the hero of Holland! The brave boy who saved our land!"

But Peter did not think of himself as a hero. He had done what he thought was right. He was glad that he could do something for the country he loved so much.

MEET NORMA GREEN, AUTHOR

Norma Green says that more than a hundred years ago, an American woman named Mary Mapes Dodge told this story to her children, making it up as she went along. It was first published in her book Hans Brinker, or The Silver Skates.

The story became so famous that the Dutch people put up a statue of Peter in a little town called Spaarndam.

Green says, "I felt there was a need today for young people to read about courage and pride in country. This story seemed to be a way of passing on these messages in a memorable fantasy."

MOLLY THE BRAVE AND ME

Jane O'Connor

illustrated by Sheila Hamanaka

Molly has guts. She has more guts than anybody in the second grade. She can stand at the top of the monkey bars on one foot.

She doesn't mind it when Nicky hides dead water bugs in her desk.

And if big kids pick on her, Molly tells them to get lost. Molly is so brave. I wish I was like her.

Today on the lunch line Molly said to me, "Beth, can you come to our house in the country this weekend? It is lots of fun there."

Wow! I guess Molly really likes me. That made me feel good.

But I have never been away from home. What if I get homesick? What if they eat stuff I don't like?

What if there are lots of wild animals? I was not sure I wanted to go.

I sat at a table with Molly. I said, "Gee, Molly. It sounds neat. Only I don't know if my parents will say yes."

That night Molly's mom called my mom. My mom said yes. So how could I say no? It was all set. Molly's parents were going to pick me up on Saturday morning.

Friday night I packed my stuff. Later my mom tucked me in bed. "I'm scared I'll miss you," I said. "I bet I'll cry all the time. Then Molly will think I'm a big baby. And she won't like me anymore."

My mom hugged me. "You will have fun. And Molly will understand if you are a little homesick." Then my

mom kissed me two times. "One kiss is for tonight. The other is for tomorrow night when you will be at Molly's house."

Molly's parents came early the next morning. I was scared, but I was excited, too. Most of all I did not want to look like a wimp around Molly. So I waved good-bye to my parents and hopped in the back seat.

Molly's dog sat between us. "This is Butch," said Molly. Right away Butch started licking me. I'm kind of scared of big dogs.

But did I show it? No way! I acted like I loved getting dog spit all over my face!

By noon we got to Molly's house. It sat all alone at the top of a hill. "This was once a farm," Molly's mom told me. "It's 150 years old."

I like new houses. They haven't had time to get any ghosts. But I didn't say that to Molly's mom.

Right after lunch we went berry picking. That sounded like fun. Then I saw all the beetles on the bushes.

I did not want to touch them. But Molly just swatted them away. So I gave it a try too. "Hey! this is fun," I said. "I have never picked food before."

We ate lots and lots of berries. Red juice got all over my face and hands. I pretended it was blood and I was a vampire.

I chased Molly all around. "You know what?" I told her. "I am really glad that I came to your house."

Later we went looking for wild flowers. That sounded nice and safe to me. We walked all the way down to a stream. A big log lay across the stream.

Molly ran right across it. Boy, what guts! Butch ran across too. I stared at the log. "Aren't there any wild flowers on this side?" I asked.

Molly shook her head. "The best ones are over here. Come on, Beth. Don't be scared. Just walk across—it's easy."

"Okay," I told myself. "Quit acting like a wimp." I started taking tiny steps across the log. Near the end I slipped.

Oof! Down I went. "Are you all right?" Molly asked.

I nodded, but my backside really hurt.

We picked flowers for a while. And when we left, I crawled across the log. Molly didn't tease me. Still I knew I looked like a jerk.

On the way back to the house Butch saw a rabbit and chased it into a field of corn. "Dumb dog!" said Molly. "He will never catch that rabbit. We'd better go and find him."

"Oh, rats!" I thought, but I went in after Molly. We followed the sound of Butch's barks. Boy, was that field big! The corn was way over our heads and it seemed to go on for miles.

At last we spotted Butch. Molly ran and hugged him. Then she pulled me by the arm. "This place is creepy," Molly said. "Let's get out of here."

That was fine with me! But it was not so easy getting out. All the corn looked the same. It was hot and hard to see. Bugs kept flying in our faces. It felt like we were walking around and around in circles.

"Can't Butch help us find the way?" I asked.

Molly shook her head. "Butch can't find his own doghouse."

Then Molly started blinking hard. And her nose got all runny. "Beth," she said. "We're really stuck in here. I'm scared."

Molly scared? I could not believe it! I held her hand. "Don't be scared," I told her, even though I was scared too. "We'll get out of here."

Then I got an idea. "Come on," I told Molly. I started to walk down the space between two rows of corn. I did not make any turns. I stayed in a straight line.

"Pretend this is a long street," I said. "Sooner or later we have to come to the end of it."

And at last we did! Molly and I hugged each other and jumped up and down. Woof! Woof! went Butch. "Hot stuff!" said Molly. "You got us out."

When we got back to Molly's house, her mother said, "Where have you girls been? It is almost time for dinner." Molly told her parents about following Butch into the corn. Then she put her arm around me.

"I was scared stiff," Molly told them. "But Beth wasn't scared at all. Boy, does she have guts!"

Guts? Me? I couldn't believe my ears!

Dinner was great. We cooked hot dogs on sticks over a fire.

And there was plenty of corn on the cob. "Oh, no! Not corn!" Molly and I shouted together. But we each ate three ears anyway.

Right before bed I did get a little homesick. Molly's mom gave me a big hug. That helped.

Then Molly told me I was her best friend. We locked pinkies on it. That helped too.

Maybe Molly was right. Maybe I really am a kid with guts!

THE LEGEND OF THE BLUEBONNET
retold and illustrated by Tomie dePaola

"Great Spirits, the land is dying. Your People are dying, too," the long line of dancers sang. "Tell us what we have done to anger you. End this drought. Save your People. Tell us what we must do so you will send the rain that will bring back life."

For three days, the dancers danced to the sound of the drums, and for three days, the People called Comanche watched and waited. And even though the hard winter was over, no healing rains came.

Drought and famine are hardest on the very young and the very old.

Among the few children left was a small girl named She-Who-Is-Alone. She sat by herself watching the dancers. In her lap was a doll made from buckskin—a warrior doll. The eyes, nose and mouth were painted on with the juice of berries. It wore beaded leggings and a belt of polished bone. On its head were brilliant blue feathers from the bird who cries "Jay-jay-jay." She loved her doll very much.

"Soon," She-Who-Is-Alone said to her doll, "the shaman will go off alone to the top of the hill to listen for the words of the Great Spirits. Then, we will know what to do so that once more the rains will come and the Earth will be green and alive. The buffalo will be plentiful and the People will be rich again."

41

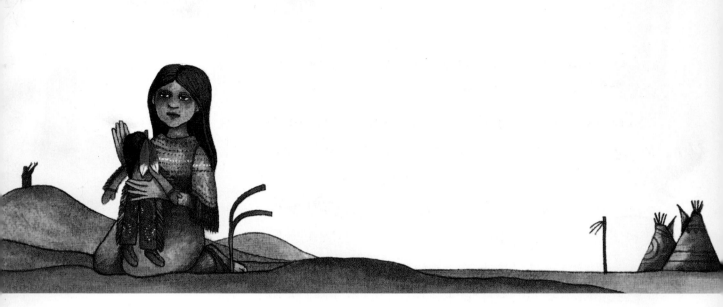

As she talked, she thought of the mother who made the doll, of the father who brought the blue feathers. She thought of the grandfather and the grandmother she had never known. They were all like shadows. It seemed long ago that they had died from the famine. The People had named her and cared for her. The warrior doll was the only thing she had left from those distant days.

"The sun is setting," the runner called as he ran through the camp. "The shaman is returning."

The People gathered in a circle and the shaman spoke. "I have heard the words of the Great Spirits," he said. "The People have become selfish. For years, they have taken from the Earth without giving anything back. The Great Spirits say the People must sacrifice. We must make a burnt offering of the most valued possession among us. The ashes of this offering shall then be scattered to the four points of the Earth, the Home of the Winds. When this sacrifice is made, drought and famine will cease. Life will be restored to the Earth and to the People!"

The People sang a song of thanks to the Great Spirits for telling them what they must do.

"I'm sure it is not my new bow that the Great Spirits want," a warrior said. "Or my special blanket," a woman added, as everyone went to their tipis to talk and think over what the Great Spirits had asked.

Everyone, that is, except She-Who-Is-Alone. She held her doll tightly to her heart. "You," she said, looking at the doll. "You are my most valued possession. It is you the Great Spirits want." And she knew what she must do.

As the council fires died out and the tipi flaps began to close, the small girl returned to the tipi, where she slept, to wait.

The night outside was still except for the distant sound of the night bird with the red wings. Soon everyone in the tipi was asleep, except She-Who-Is-Alone. Under the ashes of the tipi fire one stick still glowed. She took it and quietly crept out into the night.

She ran to the place on the hill where the Great Spirits had spoken to the shaman. Stars filled the sky, but there was no moon. "O Great Spirits," She-Who-Is-Alone said, "here is my warrior doll. It is the only thing I have from my family who died in this famine. It is my most valued possession. Please accept it."

Then, gathering twigs, she started a fire with the glowing firestick. The small girl watched as the twigs began to catch and burn.

She thought of her grandmother and grandfather, her mother and father and all the People—their suffering, their hunger. And before she could change her mind, she thrust the doll into the fire.

She watched until the flames died down and the ashes had grown cold. Then, scooping up a handful, She-Who-Is-Alone scattered the ashes to the Home of the Winds, the North and the East, the South and the West.

And there she fell asleep until the first light of the
morning sun woke her.

She looked out over the hill, and stretching out from
all sides, where the ashes had fallen, the ground was
covered with flowers—beautiful flowers, as blue as the
feathers in the hair of the doll, as blue as the feathers of
the bird who cries "Jay-jay-jay."

When the People came out of their tipis, they could scarcely believe their eyes. They gathered on the hill with She-Who-Is-Alone to look at the miraculous sight. There was no doubt about it, the flowers were a sign of forgiveness from the Great Spirits.

And as the People sang and danced their thanks to the Great Spirits, a warm rain began to fall and the land began to live again.

From that day on, the little girl was known by another name— "One-Who-Dearly-Loved-Her-People."

And every spring, the Great Spirits remember the
sacrifice of a little girl and fill the hills and valleys of the
land, now called Texas, with the beautiful blue flowers.

Even to this very day.

49 🌸

MEET TOMIE dePAOLA,
AUTHOR AND ILLUSTRATOR

*Tomie dePaola says that even though the legend of the
bluebonnet is a tale about the origin of a flower, for him it
is more a tale of the courage and sacrifice of a young
person. She-Who-Is-Alone's act of throwing her beloved
doll into the fire to save her people is the kind of action that
many young people can take, the kind of action that
creates miracles.*

FINE ART
BEING BRAVE

Brave Dog. 1979. Maurie Kerrigan.

Fresco, ceramic, aluminum foil, and painted wood. Gift of Wallace and Wilhelmina Holladay,
The National Museum of Women in the Arts, Washington, D.C.

The Life-Line. 1884. Winslow Homer.

Oil on canvas. The George W. Elkins Collection, Philadelphia Museum of Art

Warrior chief, warriors, and attendants. 16th–17th century.
Bini people, from the palace in Benin City, Nigeria.

Brass plaque. Gift of Mr. and Mrs. Klaus G. Perls, 1990, The Metropolitan Museum of Art.
1990.332. Photo: © 1991 The Metropolitan Museum of Art

SALLY RIDE, ASTRONAUT
AN AMERICAN FIRST
June Behrens

T he rocket engines roar as *Challenger* leaves the launchpad. Over half a million people are at Cape Canaveral, Florida, to watch. In less than three minutes the spacecraft is thirty miles up. Soon it disappears from sight.

This is the second flight of *Challenger*. It carries a crew of five. Aboard is mission specialist Sally Ride, age thirty-two. She is a pioneer, the first American woman in space. Sally Ride is also the youngest American astronaut to circle the earth in a spacecraft.

On the flight deck Sally Ride sits in the middle seat. She is just behind Commander Robert Crippin and Pilot Rick Hauck. Mission specialists John Fabian and Dr. Norman Thagard are also in their places. These astronauts are a team with an important mission.

Sally checks on one of the experiments that was conducted while the *Challenger* was orbiting the earth.
NASA

The spacecraft is in orbit minutes after lift-off. *Challenger* orbits, or travels once around the earth, every ninety minutes. In one day the space crew orbits the earth sixteen times.

There is important work to do aboard the spacecraft. The astronaut team runs scientific experiments. Two satellites are put into orbit. Astronaut Sally Ride works a fifty-foot robot arm. This is the first time it has been used in space.

A camera on an unmanned, free-flying shuttle satellite photographed the *Challenger* with its cargo bay empty. Later, using the robot arm, Sally retrieved a satellite from space and moved it into the cargo bay for its return to earth.
NASA

On future missions the robot arm will pick up satellites in trouble and repair them. Then the arm will return them to space.

The five astronauts complete their mission in six days. They have traveled 2.5 million miles. They return to earth, landing on the Mohave Desert in California.

About one hundred miles from the Mohave Desert is the town of Encino. Sally Ride and her younger sister Karen, nicknamed "Bear," grew up in Encino. Her parents, Dale and Joyce Ride, live there. Dr. Ride is an educator, the assistant to the president and superintendent at Santa Monica College. Mrs. Ride was a teacher at one time.

Sally knew she could do anything she wanted to do when she was a little girl growing up in Encino. Sally believed in herself. She had the will of a winner in school and in sports.

The neighborhood boys knew they'd have stiff competition in their baseball and football games when Sally was on the field. She was as good as any of them. Sally worked and played to make her team the best.

Sally was nine when Dr. Ride took a leave from his work in the schools. For a year the family traveled in Europe. Sally and her sister "Bear," aged seven, saw just how big the world is. What a great adventure, learning about other people in other countries!

After the family came home from Europe, Sally took up tennis. She knew that a winner must work hard.

Sally worked hard and played hard on the tennis court. She became the eighteenth ranked junior player in the United States. Sally worked just as hard in the classroom. She was determined to do her best in whatever she tried.

Sally Ride went to high school at Westlake School for Girls. She was one of the top six in her graduating class and a year younger than her classmates.

Sally Ride's favorite subject was science. She remembers her science teacher as an important influence in her life.

Tennis was one of the sports Sally enjoyed. Sally (center front) is pictured here with her tennis teammates.
Harvard-Westlake School

In college Sally studied the science of stars and planets called astrophysics. She was interested in great books and literature. Sally was graduated from Stanford University with two degrees, one in English and one in astrophysics.

Sally Ride continued her studies. At Stanford University she earned the master's and doctoral degrees in astrophysics. She was now Dr. Sally Ride.

One day at school Sally Ride saw an ad in a newspaper. Men and women were wanted for the space program. They would be trained to become astronauts.

Sally Ride was one of 8,900 people who wanted to be in the NASA astronaut training program. NASA is short for National Aeronautics and Space Administration. NASA looked for winners, people who were the best in their fields. Just 35 of the 8,900 applicants were chosen for the NASA astronaut class of 1978. Sally Ride was one of the six women chosen.

Sally is pictured here jogging on the Stanford University campus.

Chuck Painter/Stanford University News Service

In a simulation exercise (left), Sally learned
how it feels when the pilot's seat is ejected out of a jet.
Sally (above) is ready to depart from Houston to the
Kennedy Space Station in Florida.

Sally Ride moved from her school in California to
the Johnson Space Center in Houston, Texas. This is
the control center for NASA spacecraft missions and
astronaut training programs.

Before she knew it, Sally Ride was back in the
classroom again. Her classes were in basic astronaut
training. She had to know all about computer systems
and the hundreds of switches that control a
spacecraft. In space shuttle training she practiced
spacecraft launching and entry. Sally Ride became a
flight engineer and a pilot.

The training was hard work, physically and mentally. Sally Ride spent two years developing and working with the robot arm, which would be used on the spacecraft.

During on-the-ground training exercises Sally watched the robot arm move cargo in and out of the shuttle's cargo bay through the overhead window.
NASA

Sally Ride served twice as a capsule communicator at Mission Operations Control Center in Houston. A capsule communicator talks and relays instructions to astronauts in orbit on space flights.

The best-qualified people were chosen for the second *Challenger* mission. NASA officials wanted team players, people who could work well together. Sally Ride would be a member of that team.

59 🦂

When astronauts Joe Engle and Richard Truly flew the space shuttle *Columbia* in earth orbit, Sally served on the mission control team at the Johnson Space Center in Houston.
NASA

The photograph shows what the earth would look like to Sally Ride from her spacecraft. The photo shows a view of Lim Fjord in northern Denmark. It was taken by a satellite from 181 miles in space.

U.S. Geological Survey

Sally remembered those early travels in faraway countries. Soon Sally would be looking down at the earth from 185 miles in space. She would be passing over those countries of the world ninety-six times.

Back at Houston Sally Ride and her team worked to make the mission a success. They did in training all the things they would be doing as their spacecraft orbited the earth.

When *Challenger* lifted off the pad at Kennedy Space Center in Cape Canaveral, the world watched. Everyone listened as the astronaut team reported activities to Mission Control in Houston.

Six days later, *Challenger's* second mission touched down to a happy landing on the California desert. Sally Ride had made history. She had become the first American woman to orbit the earth. Her determination and hard work had made her a part of the winning team.

"The thing that I'll remember most about the flight is that it was fun," said Sally Ride. "In fact, I'm sure it was the most fun that I will ever have in my life."

NASA

61

The *Challenger* glided to a safe landing at Edwards Air Force Base in southern California.

NASA

BIBLIOGRAPHY

Brave Irene by William Steig. Read this exciting story about Irene, who is caught in a snowstorm while trying to deliver a dress that her mother has sewn. Will she make it through the storm?

Harry and the Terrible Whatzit by Dick Gackenbach. Read about Harry, who is afraid of the cellar until one day he ventures down to find his mother. What happens to Harry?

Monster Tracks? by A. Delaney. A boy walking through the woods is afraid of what is chasing him through the snow. Then he makes a happy discovery.

Owl Moon by Jane Yolen. In this wonderful story, a father and daughter walk in the woods to go owl-watching. Discover how the child is brave.

Peter and the Wolf by Sergei Prokofiev, translated by Maria Carlson. How will Peter catch the big, bad wolf with the help of a little bird? Read this wonderful story that was set to music by the famous composer Prokofiev.

Seven in One Blow retold by Michael Foreman and Freire Wright. Everyone admires the little tailor who swatted seven giants with one blow. He is the bravest of all. Or is he?

Storm in the Night by Mary Stolz. How does a young boy handle his fear of a storm? He does it with help, of course. This wonderful story tells how.

What's Under My Bed? by James Stevenson. Two children are afraid of the dark until, together with their grandfather, they learn what makes them afraid.

RICH AND POOR

THE THREE WISHES

retold by Anna Holst
illustrated by Ellen Joy Sasaki

Once upon a time, a man and a woman lived by the forest. They were woodcutters. Every day they went into the forest, where they worked long and hard. They cut down trees, cut them into logs, and carried the logs home to sell for firewood. But no matter how long and hard they worked, there were times that they did not earn enough money to buy good food to eat.

One day while they were working in the forest they noticed a huge oak tree.

"That tree is so big that we can cut many, many logs from it," said the woman. "We could sell the logs for a lot of money."

The man raised his ax and swung at the tree as hard as he could. No sooner did the ax hit the tree than the man and woman heard the saddest voice they had ever heard. Suddenly a tiny woman was standing in front of them.

"Oh, please," she cried. "Please don't cut down my tree."

They were so surprised that they could not say anything at first. But finally they agreed to leave the tree alone.

"To thank you for your kindness, I will grant your next three wishes, whatever they are," said the tiny woman. Then, as suddenly as she had appeared, she disappeared.

"We should think carefully about these wishes," said the man.

"Yes," agreed his wife. "I think we should go home so we can sit down and talk about it."

So they started to walk. But they were a long way from home, and after a while the man stopped. "You know," he said, "we could wish for a horse and wagon to carry the wood in."

"That's so," his wife said. Then they walked some more.

Then the woman stopped. "You know," she said, "we could wish for a big house with a fine garden."

"That's so," her husband said. Then they walked some more.

Because they stopped and talked every time they had another idea for a wish, it took much longer than usual to get home. They settled down to talk about their three wishes. They remembered all the ideas they had talked about on the way home.

"We could wish for a horse and wagon," said the man.

"We could wish for a big house," said the woman.

"Or a bag full of money!"

"Or a box of jewels!"

"We could wish never to be hungry again," said the man.

"That would be good," said the woman.

"To tell you the truth, I'm hungry now," said the man. "Isn't it time to eat?"

"Not yet," said the woman.

"But I'm so hungry," he said. "I wish I had a great big plate of sausages!"

In a flash, a big plate appeared in front of him, piled high with sausages.

"Oh, no! You've wasted one of our wishes!" cried the woman. "How could you be so stupid? I wish those sausages were hanging from your nose!"

In a flash, the sausages were hanging from her husband's nose.

"Now who's stupid?" said the man. "You've wasted the second wish! Now we have only one wish left."

The man pulled and pulled at the sausages. They stuck tight to his nose. The woman pulled and pulled at the sausages. Still they stuck tight to the man's nose.

The man and woman together pulled and pulled and
pulled at the sausages. They stuck and stuck and stuck
to his nose.

Finally, the man said, "There's only one thing to do."

So together they wished that the sausages would
come off his nose.

In a flash, the sausages were piled on the dish on
the table.

Well, the man and woman didn't have a horse and
wagon or a big house or a bag full of money or a box of
jewels, but at least they had the best plate of sausages
they had ever eaten!

THE GOOSE THAT LAID THE GOLDEN EGGS

Aesop

illustrated by Rowan Barnes-Murphy

Once upon a time a man and a woman lived on a small farm. They worked hard, but they did not make much money.

One day the man said to his wife, "Are you happy?"

"Oh, yes," she said. "We do not have much money, but we have everything we need."

The next morning the man went to milk the cow, just as he always did. His wife went to gather the eggs that the chickens and the goose had laid, just as she always did. Suddenly the man heard his wife calling out.

He ran to see what she wanted.

"Look!" she cried. "The goose has laid a golden egg!"

Sure enough, the woman was holding an egg made of solid gold.

"How wonderful!" said the man. "Now we can buy a new wagon."

So the man went into town, sold the golden egg, and bought a new wagon.

The very next morning, the man was milking when he heard his wife call out again.

"Look!" she cried. "Another one!"

In her hand was another egg, and again, it was made of solid gold.

"How wonderful!" said the man. "Now we can buy some new tools."

So the man went into town, sold the golden egg, and bought some new tools.

73

Every morning, the goose laid another golden egg, and every day the man and his wife bought more and more lovely things for themselves. They hired helpers to do all the work on the farm.

Then one night the man said, "You know, if we had a lot of those golden eggs at the same time, we would be rich."

The woman said, "How wonderful! I've always wanted to be rich!"

"The eggs must be inside the goose," said the man. "If we cut her open, we can get all the eggs we want."

"Oh, yes!" cried the woman. "What are we waiting for? We will be rich!"

Before you could blink, the man got his ax and cut open the goose, and what do you think he found? Inside, the goose was just like any other goose.

The next morning, the man said, "We used to be happy."

"Then we got greedy," said his wife, "and now we have killed the goose that laid the golden eggs!"

Then the man went to milk the cow, just as he used to do. His wife went to gather the eggs that the chickens had laid, just as she used to do.

THE EMPTY POT
Demi

A long time ago in China there was a boy named Ping who loved flowers. Anything he planted burst into bloom. Up came flowers, bushes, and even big fruit trees, as if by magic!

Everyone in the kingdom loved flowers too. They planted them everywhere, and the air smelled like perfume.

The Emperor loved birds and animals, but flowers most of all, and he tended his own garden every day. But the Emperor was very old. He needed to choose a successor to the throne.

Who would his successor be? And how would the Emperor choose? Because the Emperor loved flowers so much, he decided to let the flowers choose.

The next day a proclamation was issued: All the children in the land were to come to the palace. There they would be given special flower seeds by the Emperor. "Whoever can show me their best in a year's time," he said, "will succeed me to the throne."

This news created great excitement throughout the land! Children from all over the country swarmed to the palace to get their flower seeds. All the parents wanted their children to be chosen Emperor, and all the children hoped they would be chosen too!

When Ping received his seed from the Emperor, he was the happiest child of all. He was sure he could grow the most beautiful flower.

Ping filled a flowerpot with rich soil. He planted the seed in it very carefully.

He watered it every day. He couldn't wait to see it sprout, grow, and blossom into a beautiful flower!

Day after day passed, but nothing grew in his pot.

Ping was very worried. He put new soil into a bigger pot. Then he transferred the seed into the rich black soil.

Another two months he waited. Still nothing happened.

By and by the whole year passed.

Spring came, and all the children put on their best clothes to greet the Emperor.

They rushed to the palace with their beautiful flowers, eagerly hoping to be chosen.

Ping was ashamed of his empty pot. He thought the other children would laugh at him because for once he couldn't get a flower to grow.

His clever friend ran by, holding a great big plant. "Ping!" he said. "You're not really going to the Emperor with an empty pot, are you? Couldn't you grow a great big flower like mine?"

"I've grown lots of flowers better than yours," Ping said. "It's just this seed that won't grow."

Ping's father overheard this and said, "You did your best, and your best is good enough to present to the Emperor."

Holding the empty pot in his hands, Ping went straight away to the palace.

The Emperor was looking at the flowers slowly, one by one.

How beautiful all the flowers were!

But the Emperor was frowning and did not say a word.

Finally he came to Ping. Ping hung his head in shame, expecting to be punished.

The Emperor asked him, "Why did you bring an empty pot?"

Ping started to cry and replied, "I planted the seed you gave me and I watered it every day, but it didn't sprout. I put it in a better pot with better soil, but still it didn't sprout! I tended it all year long, but nothing grew. So today I had to bring an empty pot without a flower. It was the best I could do."

When the Emperor heard these words, a smile slowly spread over his face, and he put his arm around Ping. Then he exclaimed to one and all, "I have found him! I have found the one person worthy of being Emperor!

"Where you got your seeds from, I do not know. For the seeds I gave you had all been cooked. So it was impossible for any of them to grow.

"I admire Ping's great courage to appear before me with the empty truth, and now I reward him with my entire kingdom and make him Emperor of all the land!"

83

MEET DEMI, AUTHOR AND ILLUSTRATOR

Charlotte Dumaresq Hunt uses her childhood nickname, Demi, as her pen name. She studied art in several schools, but much of Demi's learning took place as she traveled to faraway places, such as Brazil, India, and China. The Empty Pot shows the influence of China on Demi's learning.

Demi has not limited her art to children's books. She has made prints that hang in museums in the United States and India. She has painted wall murals in Mexico and the dome of a church in California.

CINDERELLA
Charles Perrault
translated by Fabio Coen
illustrated by Rosekrans Hoffman

Once there was a girl who was very kind and patient. Her wicked stepmother called her Cinderella because she often sat by the fireplace close to the cinders.

Her stepmother made her work all day long. She had
to light the fire, prepare the meals, wash the dishes,
clean the house, and make beautiful gowns for her two
stepsisters, who were very ugly and very mean.

Cinderella was always dressed in rags, but she was
more beautiful in her rags than her stepsisters in their
beautiful gowns.

One day the King and Queen gave a ball. Cinderella helped her stepmother and her stepsisters to get ready. Then the three of them went to the ball.

Cinderella was all alone. She began to cry. Suddenly her Fairy Godmother appeared. "Why are you crying?" she asked Cinderella.

"I, too, would have liked to go to the ball," Cinderella replied.

"Then you shall go," said her Fairy Godmother. "Bring me a pumpkin from the garden."

With one touch of her magic wand, Cinderella's Fairy Godmother turned the pumpkin into a beautiful carriage. Then she took six mice from a trap. A touch of the magic wand turned them into six prancing horses. In the cellar Cinderella's Fairy Godmother found a large rat. She turned him into a large coachman with a great mustache.

Another touch of the magic wand and Cinderella's rags turned into a beautiful silver gown covered with diamonds. On her feet were a pair of little glass slippers.

As she stepped into the carriage, her Fairy Godmother said, "Have a good time, but remember this. You must leave the ball before midnight. When the clock strikes twelve, your carriage will turn into a pumpkin, your horses into mice, your coachman into a rat, and your gown into rags."

Cinderella promised to leave the ball before midnight. Then they drove away.

Cinderella was so beautiful that the prince danced with her all night. She forgot about her Fairy Godmother's warning. The clock began to strike twelve. Cinderella ran out of the palace and down the stairs. In her hurry she lost one of her glass slippers.

The prince ran after Cinderella, but it was too late. By the time he reached the bottom of the stairs, her beautiful carriage was gone. The prince found only her little glass slipper.

The prince had fallen in love with Cinderella. He wanted to find her, but he didn't even know her name or where she lived. He sent a page to every house in the kingdom. In each house the page asked every girl to try on the slipper. But their feet were much too big for the tiny slipper. At last the page came to the house where Cinderella lived. Her two stepsisters hurried to try on the little slipper. But their feet were much too big. No matter how hard they tried, they could not get the slipper on.

Then it was Cinderella's turn. The slipper fit her perfectly. At that moment her Fairy Godmother appeared and dressed Cinderella in a gown of shimmering gold.

Cinderella and the prince were married. Because she was so kind, Cinderella forgave her wicked stepmother and stepsisters, and they all lived happily ever after.

THE SIMPLE PRINCE

Jane Yolen
illustrated by Jack Kent

There was once a prince who longed to live a simple life. He was tired of idle foolishness and fancy dress balls.

So he clapped his hands three times to call his servants.

"Bring me some plain clothes," he demanded. "I am going out into the world to live the simple life."

The servants found a plain suit and a plain hat as well.

The prince clapped his hands three times and ordered a simple picnic lunch to eat on his way.

93

Then he rode off to find the simple life.

He rode for many hours until at last he came to the house of a poor farmer.

"If I cannot live the simple life here," said the prince, "then I cannot live it anywhere."

He got off his horse and went to the door. He clapped his hands three times. Nothing happened.

He snapped his fingers. He tapped his toes.

At last he grew impatient.
"Open up," he ordered.
The door was opened.
The farmer looked out.

"I have come to live the
simple life," said the prince.
He walked inside.

95

The farmer stared at his
wife. She stared at the prince.
The prince did not notice.

Instead he went around the
room with his handkerchief to

his nose. "What an awful smell," said the prince.
"Is this what comes from living the simple life?"

"No!" said the farmer's wife. "It comes from
making cheese."

"Cheese!" said the prince. He sat down on a
stool and clapped his hands three times.

"I want some cheese. And a cup of tea to go with it. I have been on the road so long looking for the simple life, I am quite starved."

The farmer looked at his wife. She shook her head. "No good will come of this," she said. The farmer just smiled.

He cut the prince a slice of cheese. Then he said, "Cheese and tea. That is simple. Here is the cheese.

"But as for the tea, we need fire and water. First I must saw the wood for the fire. It is simple. Come with me."

The prince went outside with the farmer. They found some wood. They sawed, and they sawed, and they sawed some more.

The woodpile grew bigger and bigger. At last the prince cried out, "Enough! Enough! I can do no more."

"We are done," said the farmer.

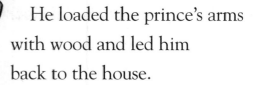

He loaded the prince's arms with wood and led him back to the house.

Then the farmer made the
fire. The prince sat down again.
"Now it is time to get the water,"
said the farmer's wife. "It is
simple. Come with me."

So the prince followed the
farmer's wife to the well. Arm
over arm, he pulled the bucket
up. He poured the bucket into a
pitcher. One bucket. Then
another. Then a third.

At last the prince cried, "Enough! Enough! I can do no more."

"We are done," said the farmer's wife. She gave the prince a pitcher for each hand. She put another on his head. Then she led him back to the house.

The farmer's wife poured the water into the kettle and put the kettle on the fire. When it was hot she made the tea.

But the prince was twice as hungry as before.

The prince clapped his hands three times. "Bring me some bread and butter with my tea."

"That is simple enough," said the farmer. "But butter begins with milk, and milk comes from a cow. Come along with me."

So the prince followed the farmer to the barn. There he held the pail while the farmer milked the cow.

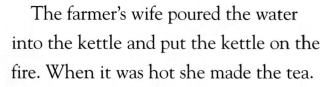

99

The cow's tail hit the prince's face. The cow's hooves kicked the prince's knees. At last the prince cried, "Enough! Enough! I can do no more."

"It is done," said the farmer.

Back in the house, the farmer made the prince churn, and churn, and churn the milk into butter. When it was done, the prince fell back on the stool. He clapped his hands feebly three times. "My butter needs some bread," he said.

"That is simple," said the farmer's wife. "But first we must bake it. Come along to help."

So she rolled up the prince's sleeves and gave him a big lump of dough.

He kneaded it. He patted it. He punched it. At last he cried, "Enough! Enough! I can do no more."

"It's done," said the farmer's wife, and she put the dough into the oven to bake.

But the prince was so tired from sawing and hauling, from milking and churning, from kneading and pounding, that he fell fast asleep. He slept through the bread-baking and dinner, and did not wake up until morning. He felt stiff and tired and cranky. He tried to clap his hands—one time, two times, three times. But his hands were much too sore from all the work he had done.

"Please," he said weakly, "may I have something to eat?"

"It's simple," the wife began. But before she could finish, the prince jumped up from the stool. "Enough! Enough!" he cried. "I can live no more of the simple life. It is much too hard for me!"

He ran out the door, climbed on his horse, and galloped back to the castle as fast as he could go.

His servants helped him off his horse, and the grateful prince said, "Thank you."

Then he asked, "Please, may I have some porridge? I am quite starved."

His servants rejoiced at being treated so politely and went quickly to fetch the porridge and a pitcher of fresh milk.

And from that day to this, the prince lived happily, never again clapping his hands for anything.

Instead, he was always careful to say "please" and "thank you." It was so much simpler that way.

FINE ART
RICH AND POOR

Golden litter of the Lord Inca.
Date unknown.

Manuscript illustration. Private collection.
Photo: American Heritage Library.

The Third-Class Carriage. c. 1862.
Honoré Daumier.

Oil on canvas. The H.O. Havemeyer Collection, 1929,
The Metropolitan Museum of Art. 29.100.129. Photo: © 1985
The Metropolitan Museum of Art

The Maids of Honor. 1656. Diego Velázquez.

Oil on canvas. Museo del Prado, Madrid. Photo: SCALA/Art Resource

AMADOU'S STORY

Linda Robbins
illustrated by Marcy Ramsey

My name is Amadou. I live in the village of N'Dimb. When I am grown, I shall be a great storyteller. That is because I honor storytellers more than anyone else—even more than I honor the elders who are the wisest people in our village. Now I would like to tell you a story about N'Dimb.

The place called N'Dimb is hard, but it is not a bad place to live. It is true that it is near the desert and that we cannot always count on the rains. When there is not much rain, we cannot grow much food. It is also true that our work is very hard. Yet, the hard work gives us food to eat together at night. And that is very, very good.

A few years ago, the people in my village often knew great hunger. When there was enough rain, our favorite grain—millet—grew well and we ate like kings. However, when there was no rain, millet did not grow well and we were often hungry.

And the times without rain were sometimes very long. There would be so little food that the older children would leave N'Dimb and go far away to the city to try to find work.

When there was much rain and farmers had more than enough grain, they had extra to sell. But there was a problem. When one farmer had good crops, so did all the others. Then nobody really needed to buy grain. But the rich people could afford to buy the extra grain and store it for a long time. Later, in times without rain, everyone needed to buy grain. Then the rich could make people pay a lot of money for the stored grain—more money than most people had. So most of them kept getting poorer.

Then, one day, the wise elders got together to see what could be done. They knew that together the people of N'Dimb could solve this difficult problem. They knew that "two eyes see better than one." There were many more than two eyes willing to look for answers.

The elders of our village talked to the wise elders of the city of Dakar. The elders of Dakar knew other wise people in a far-off country. All of this wisdom was very powerful indeed.

107

The people learned much from this combined wisdom. Sometimes this strange mixture of ideas caused arguments, but the elders were patient. It took time, but by talking together about their problems, the people of my village learned to do many new things together.

They learned to build strong fences to keep wild animals out of their gardens. They learned to dig canals and put in pumps to bring water up from the lake to water the vegetables. They planted big fields of millet and beans and melons to make a huge village garden. They grew more than they could eat in one season. And best of all, they learned how to store extra food in a grain bank. Now they could store food like the rich people did. This is how the people did it:

When the crops were plentiful, the elders built a big storehouse for the whole village. They called it the grain bank. The people agreed to save bags of grain in the bank when there were extra crops.

Now, working together, many people could do the same thing that one rich person could do. They could store crops until there was a dry season. And the dry season came. Once again, the fields turned brown and died. Everything turned brown except the little gardens that people could still water with their sprinkling cans.

There were not enough crops in the fields, but this time crops did not have to be bought from the rich at high prices. The grain bank opened for the first time. A blackboard was set up in the village, right in front of the storehouse. The people of the village—all the mothers and daughters and fathers and sons—came forward to buy the grain at a fair price the elders had set. Then they took it home for their families to eat.

The people of N'Dimb solved their problem. From the day the grain bank opened until this day, the people have known no hunger. People no longer keep getting poorer. They found out that learning is important. They learned that by thinking and working together, they can help each other solve problems.

That is my story of N'Dimb.

THE GOLDEN GOOSE

Jacob and Wilhelm Grimm
illustrated by Betsy Day

Once there was a man with three sons. The first two sons were strong, handsome, and clever. The third son was not strong, handsome, or clever, but he was very kind. Yet everyone made fun of him and called him Simpleton.

One day, the oldest son went
into the forest to chop wood.
His mother gave him a pancake
and some apple cider for his lunch.

In the forest, he met a little
gray man who said, "I'm so hungry!
I'm so thirsty! Could I have some of your
food and drink?"

"Of course not!" said the son.
"Then there won't be enough for me! Go away!"

He turned his back on the little gray man
and began to chop a tree. Right away he hurt
his arm, so the son went home.

The next day, the second son went into the
forest to chop wood. His mother also gave him a
pancake and some apple cider to take with him.

The little gray man showed up again and said,
"I'm so hungry! I'm so thirsty! Could I have
some of your food and drink?"

"Of course not!" said the second son. "Then
there won't be enough for me! Go away!"

He began to chop the tree. Right away he
hurt his leg, so he too had to go home. Now, all
this was the little gray man's doing.

The third day, Simpleton wanted to try his hand at chopping wood. He had to beg his father to let him do it until finally his father said yes. Simpleton's mother gave him a loaf of hard bread baked in ashes and a jug of water.

When the little gray man appeared before him in the forest and asked him for food and drink, Simpleton said, "Of course, my good man. I only have hard bread and plain water, but I will be glad to share them with you." When he unwrapped his plain bread, it had turned into a pancake! The water in the jug had turned to sweet apple cider! So Simpleton and the little gray man feasted on a great meal.

When they finished eating, the little man said, "You have a kind heart. You shared your food and drink with me. Now I will do something for you. There is an old tree over there. Cut it down and you will find something among the roots." Then the little gray man went on his way.

Simpleton did as he was told and chopped down the tree. There among the roots sat a goose with feathers of pure gold! Simpleton took the goose and went to an inn to spend the night.

The innkeeper had three daughters. When they saw the goose, they wondered what kind of magic goose it was. The oldest girl thought, "I would like to have one of its feathers. Then I would be rich." She waited until Simpleton went out of the room, then grabbed the goose to pluck one of its feathers. But her hand stuck to the goose, and she could not pull it away!

Soon the middle daughter came by. She too wanted to have a golden goose feather. Then she saw her sister stuck to the goose and tried to pull her away. She stuck to her sister!

Finally, the youngest sister came by for her goose feather. "Stay away! Don't touch us!" yelled her sisters. It was too late. She tried to pull her middle sister away and, of course, she stuck to her too! So the three daughters had to spend the night stuck to each other and to the goose.

The next morning, Simpleton took his goose and left the inn. He didn't even bother looking at the three girls stuck to the goose and running behind him. They all ran and ran, sometimes straight ahead, sometimes to the left, sometimes to the right.

In the middle of a field, they met the pastor, and when he saw the young girls running behind Simpleton, he said, "Shame on you! You shouldn't chase a young man like that!" When he tried to pull the younger daughter's hand, his hand stuck to hers!

Now the pastor was added to the parade, running behind Simpleton. In a little while, they ran into the sexton, who said to the pastor, "Where are you running to? Have you forgotten we have a service today?" He ran to the pastor to stop him. Well, the sexton grabbed the pastor's sleeve and stuck to it, and he too was running with the rest of them behind Simpleton.

As the five of them ran after Simpleton, one behind the other, they met two farmers coming out of the hayfields. The sexton shouted to them to set them free. But when the farmers touched the sexton they stuck too, one behind the other. Now there were seven people following Simpleton and his goose.

Soon they came to the town where the king lived. The king had a daughter who was very serious. She never smiled. She never laughed.

The king had said, "She will marry the man who makes her laugh."

When Simpleton heard about this, he led his parade to the princess. As soon as she saw them, the princess began to laugh and laugh and couldn't stop laughing.

"I will marry you," she said.

When the king heard this, he was not happy. He did not want his daughter to marry a man named Simpleton. The king said to him, "If you want to marry my daughter, first you have to bring me a man who can drink all the cider in my cellar."

Simpleton thought of the little gray man he met in the forest. He went looking for him. He found him sitting on the stump of the tree he had cut. The little man looked sad.

"I am so thirsty! I can't get enough to drink!" said the little man.

"I can help you," said Simpleton. "Come with me and you can drink all you want."

He took the little gray man to the king's cellar. The little gray man drank and drank all the cider in the great barrels. By the end of the day all the cider was gone.

The king then made another demand. He told Simpleton that he must bring to him a man who could eat up a mountain of bread.

Simpleton again went to look for the little gray man in the forest. He found him sitting on the stump of the tree. Again the little man looked sad.

"What is wrong now?" asked Simpleton.

"I am so hungry! I never seem to get enough to eat!"

"Then come with me," said Simpleton happily. "I will show you how you can eat and be filled!"

When they arrived at the court, there was a huge
mountain of bread that had been baked that morning.
The little gray man ate and ate. By the end of the day
the whole mountain of bread had disappeared.

Once more, the king made another demand. This time he asked Simpleton to bring him a ship that sailed on land as well as on sea.

Without wasting any time, Simpleton went to the forest to find the little gray man. When he told him what the king wanted, the little man said, "You gave me food and drink, and now I will give you the ship. I did all these things for you because you have a good heart and were kind to me."

Simpleton now had a ship that sailed by land and by sea. When the King saw Simpleton arriving in his ship, he could no longer say no.

So Simpleton married the princess. In time, he became king and ruled wisely and well.

BIBLIOGRAPHY

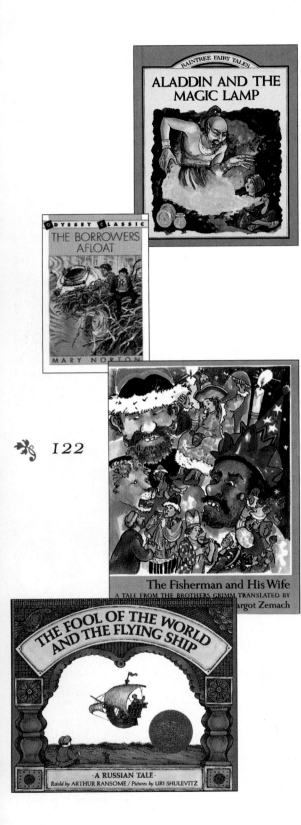

Aladdin and the Magic Lamp retold by Patricia Daniels. Read about the marvelous adventures of Aladdin, who with the help of a genie from a magic lamp fights an evil magician and wins the hand of a beautiful princess.

The Borrowers Afloat by Mary Norton. Enjoy this wonderful story about little people barely six inches high, who secretly live in other people's homes and borrow whatever they need.

The Fisherman and His Wife translated by Randall Jarrell. Find out what happens when a poor fisherman catches a fish with magic powers. He and his greedy wife learn a lesson they won't forget.

The Fool of the World and the Flying Ship retold by Arthur Ransome. A boy's good deeds allow him to get a flying ship, make new friends who have marvelous powers, overcome obstacles, marry a princess, and live happily ever after.

122

Fortune by Diane Stanley. Poor Omar spends the little money he has to buy a dancing tiger. To Omar's surprise, the tiger makes his fortune. How does he manage to do it? This funny tale tells how.

Little Sister and the Month Brothers retold by Beatrice Schenk de Regniers. Little Sister's stepmother and stepsister send her out into the snow to look for fresh violets. The twelve Month Brothers work their special magic to help Little Sister.

The Rich Man and the Shoemaker by La Fontaine. Read the story of a poor shoemaker and his rich neighbor. When the neighbor shares his money with the shoemaker, the poor man's troubles begin.

The Treasure by Uri Shulevitz. A poor man has a dream in which he is told how he can become rich. Read and find out what happens when the poor man follows the directions.

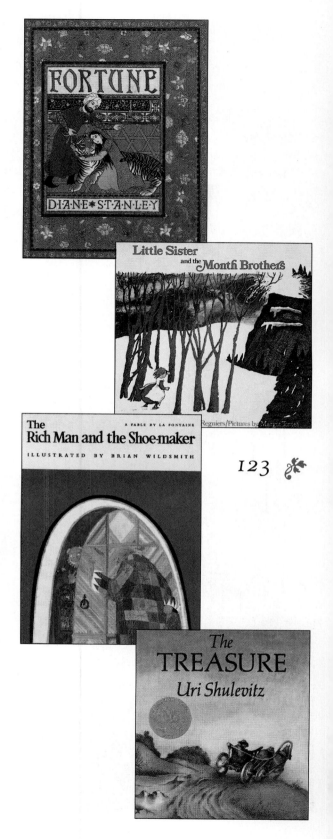

123

124

FOSSILS

125 ℯ

FOSSILS TELL OF
LONG AGO
Aliki

Once upon a time a huge fish was swimming around when
  along came a smaller fish.
The big fish was so hungry it swallowed the other fish whole.
The big fish died and sank to the bottom of the sea.

126

This happened ninety million years ago.

How do we know?

We know because the fish turned to stone.

The fish became a fossil.

A plant or animal that has turned to stone is called a fossil.

Scientists can tell how old stones are.

They could tell how old the fish fossil was.

How did the fish become a fossil?

Most animals and plants do not become fossils when they die.

Some rot.

Others dry up, crumble, and blow away.

No trace of them is left.

This could have happened to the big fish.

We would never know it had lived.

Instead, the fish became a fossil.
This is how it happened.

When the big fish died, it sank into the mud at the
  bottom of the sea.
Slowly, the soft parts of the fish rotted away.
Only its hard bones were left.
The bones of the fish it had eaten were left, too.
The skeleton of the fish lay buried and protected deep
  in the mud.
Thousands of years went by.
More layers of mud covered the fish.
Tons and tons of mud piled up.
After a long time, the surface of the earth changed.
The sea where the fish was buried dried out.
The weight of the layers of mud pressed down.
Slowly, the mud turned to rock.

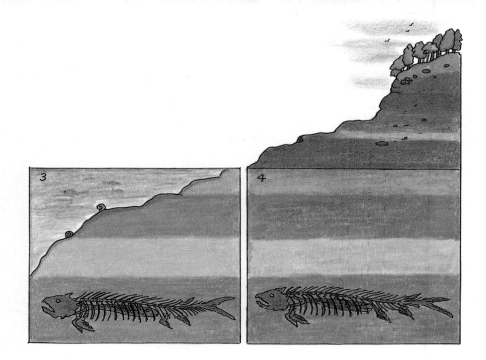

As that happened, ground water seeped through the
     changing layers of mud.
Minerals were dissolved in the water.
The water seeped into all the tiny holes in the fish bones.
The minerals in the water were left behind in the fish bones.
After a very long time the bones turned to stone.
The fish was a fossil.
Some fossils, like the fish, are actual parts of plants or
     animals that have turned to stone.
Sometimes a fossil is only an imprint of a plant or animal.

Millions of years ago, a leaf fell off a fernlike plant.

It dropped onto the swampy forest soil, which is called peat.

The leaf rotted away.

But it left the mark of its shape in the peat.

The peat, with the imprint of the leaf, hardened.

It became a rock called coal.

Coal is a fossil, too.

These are dinosaur tracks.

They were made in fresh mud 115 million years ago.

Sand filled the dinosaur's footprints in the mud.

The sand hardened into a rock called sandstone.

Millions of years later fossil hunters dug through the rock.

They found the fossil tracks—exact imprints of the
dinosaur's foot.

Not all fossils are found in stone.

Some are found in the frozen ground of the Arctic.

This ancient mammoth was a kind of elephant.

It froze to death thousands of years ago.

The grass it had been eating was still in its mouth!

Millions of years ago, a fly was caught in the sticky
    sap of a tree.
The sap hardened and became a fossil called amber.
Amber looks like yellow glass.
The fly was perfectly preserved in the amber.
Other insects have been preserved in amber, too.
We have learned many things from the fish, the fern,
    the fly, and the dinosaur tracks.
Fossils tell us about the past.

Fossils tell us there once were forests where now
    there are deserts.

Fossils tell us there once were seas where now there
    are mountains.

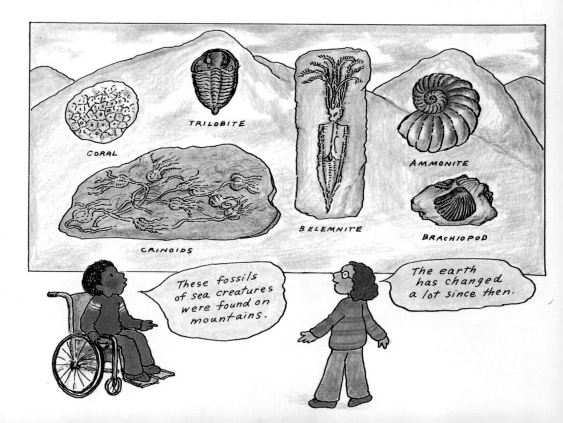

Many lands that are cold today were once warm.
We find fossils of tropical plants in very cold places.

Fossils tell us about strange creatures that lived on
    earth long ago.
No such creatures are alive today.

135

They have all died out.
We say they are extinct.

Dinosaur bones!

It's Stegosaurus!

That's Pteranodon, the flying reptile.

Here's an ichthyosaur!

It was quite a swimmer.

I love museums!

Some fossils are found by scientists who dig for them.

Some fossils are found by accident.
You, too, might find a fossil if you look hard.
When you see a stone, look at it carefully.
It may be a fossil of something that once lived.

How would you like to make a fossil?
Not a one-million-year-old fossil.
A one-minute-old fossil.
Make a clay imprint of your hand.
The imprint shows what your hand is like, the way a
 dinosaur's track shows us what its foot was like.

Suppose, when it dried out, you buried your clay imprint.
Suppose a million years from now, someone found it.
Your imprint would be as hard as stone.
It would be a fossil of your hand.
It would tell the finder something about you.
It would tell something about life on earth a million
　　years earlier.

Every time someone finds a fossil, we learn more about
life on earth long ago.
Someday you may find a fossil—one that is millions and
millions of years old.
You may discover something no one knows today.

139

MEET ALIKI, AUTHOR AND ILLUSTRATOR

Aliki likes to draw, write, grow flowers, and travel. One summer, when Aliki was in Greece with her husband and their two children, her son found a fossil of brachiopods on a dusty road. Although Aliki had been interested in fossils before, she wrote Fossils Tell of Long Ago *as a result of her son's discovery that summer.*

Aliki has written many books about fossils and other subjects, including some books written under her full name, Aliki Brandenberg.

THE DINOSAUR WHO LIVED IN MY BACKYARD

B. G. Hennessy

illustrated by Susan Davis

There used to be a dinosaur who lived in my backyard. Sometimes I wish he still lived here. The dinosaur who lived here hatched from an egg that was as big as a basketball.

By the time he was five, he was as big as our car.
Just one of his dinosaur feet was so big it wouldn't
even have fit in my sandbox.

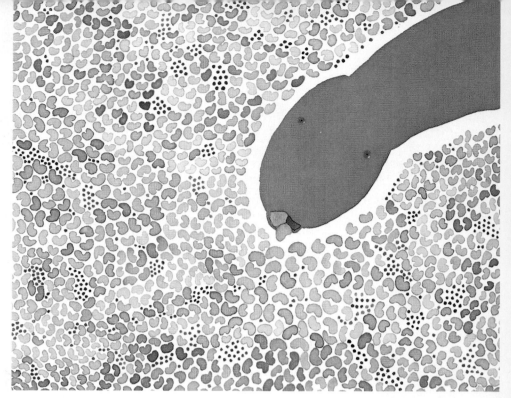

My mother says that if you eat all your vegetables you'll grow very strong. That must be true, because that's all this dinosaur ate. I bet he ate a hundred pounds of vegetables every day. That's a whole lot of lima beans.

This dinosaur was so heavy that he would have made my whole neighborhood shake like pudding if he jumped. He weighed as much as twenty pick-up trucks.

The dinosaur who lived in my backyard was bigger than my schoolbus. Even bigger than my house.

He had many other dinosaur friends. Sometimes they played hide-and-seek.

Sometimes they had terrible fights.

The dinosaur who used to live here was allowed to sleep outside every night. It's a good thing he didn't need a tent. He was so big he would have needed a circus tent to keep him covered.

Back when my dinosaur lived here, my town was a big swamp. This dinosaur needed a lot of water. If he still lived here we'd have to keep the sprinkler on all the time.

My dinosaur had a very long neck so he could eat the leaves at the top of trees. If he still lived here, I bet he could rescue my kite.

That's all I know about the dinosaur who used to live in my backyard.

He hasn't been around for a very long time. Sometimes I wish he still lived here.

It would be pretty hard to keep a dinosaur happy.

But my sister and I are saving all our lima beans—just in case.

WHY DID THE DINOSAURS DISAPPEAR?

Karen Sapp

illustrated by Bob Barner

Once dinosaurs lived on the earth. Then they disappeared. What happened to them?

Dinosaurs roamed the earth for about 140 million years. Then, 65 million years ago, they died out. So did many other animals, including animals that lived in the sea and animals that flew through the air. Many plants died too.

No one knows for sure what happened, but scientists have some ideas.

Some scientists think that new kinds of plants started growing because of changes in the climate. Their idea is that these plants poisoned dinosaurs that ate them. Then meat-eating dinosaurs starved to death when they could not find plant-eating dinosaurs to eat. There is a problem with this idea. Only land animals would have eaten the poisonous plants, but sea animals died, too. Besides, this idea does not explain why some kinds of plants also died out.

Did other animals cause the death of the dinosaurs? Maybe small animals stole and ate dinosaur eggs before they could hatch. This would explain what happened to dinosaurs that laid eggs. But what about dinosaurs that were born live? What about the sea animals and plants that died, too?

147

Many scientists think that the dinosaurs died out because the earth became very cold. Most dinosaurs could not live in very cold weather. They did not have fur or feathers to keep them warm. Dinosaurs were so huge they could not burrow into the ground for warmth and protection. But what could make the weather become so cold?

The earth long ago was not at all like it is today. Huge earthquakes made the water in the oceans rise and fall many times. When the water level fell, there was more moisture in the air. This caused more rain and colder weather. The earthquakes also made volcanoes erupt all over the world. Some scientists think that a giant volcano in the part of the world we now call India erupted for 500,000 years!

All this time, it blew so much ash and dust into the air that the sun's rays could not reach the earth. Imagine what it would be like never to see the sun! The earth grew very cold. Plants died without the sunlight. Without plants to eat, the plant-eating dinosaurs died. Then the meat-eaters died.

In 1978, a new discovery gave some scientists another idea about why the earth became so cold. Scientists found a thin layer of clay in many places all over the world. The clay is made up of dust from the time the dinosaurs were dying out. This clay has large amounts of a very rare metal, called *iridium*, that is usually deep inside the earth. When iridium is found near the earth's surface, it usually came from space, in the form of meteorites.

Meteorites are chunks of stone or metal that have crashed to the earth. Most of the time, meteorites do not hit the earth hard enough to do much damage. Sometimes, though, a very large meteorite crashes. When this happens, it makes a huge hole, or *crater*, in the ground.

In 1980, a crater was found in Mexico. Scientists think the crater was made about the time the dinosaurs disappeared. They think the meteorite that caused this crater was 6 miles long.

150

Imagine something that big hitting the earth! It would blast millions of tons of dust and rock into the sky. Heat caused by the crash would start many fires. The smoke from those fires would add soot to the air. (Scientists found large amounts of soot mixed in with the iridium.) The thick cloud of dust, rock, and smoke would swirl around the world, blocking the sunlight for months or even years. Without sunlight, the earth would grow very cold. When the dust finally settled, it would form a layer of clay, and in the clay there would be large amounts of iridium. This is exactly what some scientists think happened. Again, their idea is that the lack of sunshine caused dinosaurs and other life forms to die.

Some scientists think that both the volcano idea and the meteorite idea could be correct. There are two ways this might work. One is that a meteorite might have hit the earth hard enough to make the volcanoes erupt. Another way is that the volcanoes could have been erupting for many years, slowly killing plants and animals. Then, when a meteorite hit, it quickly finished the job.

No one really knows for sure why the dinosaurs disappeared, but many scientists are still trying to find out.

FOSSILS
Lilian Moore
illustrated by
Murray Tinkelman

Older than
books,
than scrolls,

older
than the first
tales told

or the
first words
spoken

are the stories

in forests that
turned to
stone

in ice walls
that trapped the
mammoth

in the long
bones of
dinosaurs—

the fossil
stories that begin
Once upon a time

MEET LILIAN MOORE, POET
*When Lilian Moore was growing
up, she would sit on a big box in
front of the hardware store on the
street where she lived and tell stories
to other children. As an adult,
Moore found writing stories and
poetry the easiest way to tell about
her ideas and feelings.*

*Moore believes that poetry makes us
feel good because we can read about
our feelings. It can even help us
learn about nature and science.*

153 🌿

IGUANODON
Jack Prelutsky

Iguanodon, Iguanodon,
whatever made you fade,
you've traveled on, Iguanodon,
we wish you could have stayed.

Iguanodon, Iguanodon,
we've sought you everywhere,
both here and yon, Iguanodon,
but failed to find you there.

Iguanodon, Iguanodon,
you were a gentle kind,
but now you're gone, Iguanodon,
and left your bones behind.

154

illustrated by Daniel Moreton

SEISMOSAURUS
Jack Prelutsky

Seismosaurus was enormous,
Seismosaurus was tremendous,
Seismosaurus was prodigious,
Seismosaurus was stupendous.

Seismosaurus was titanic,
Seismosaurus was colossal,
Seismosaurus now is nothing
but a monumental fossil.

155

MEET JACK PRELUTSKY, POET
*Jack Prelutsky says he tries to tell children that
poetry is one way a person can tell another person what's going
on inside him or her.*

*Prelutsky says that he began to visit schools and recite his
poetry to children because he wanted to know how his poetry
was received by the only really important audience—children.
He once said, "Poetry is as delightful and surprising as being
tickled or catching a snowflake on a mitten."*

FINE ART
FOSSILS

Fossil of an extinct ancestor of the crayfish, found in the Hummelberg Quarry, Solnhofen, Germany.

Photo: © Jonathan Blair/Woodfin Camp & Associates

 156

Dinosaur. 1980.
Mary Frank.

Color monotype, 24.75" x 35.5". Collection of Whitney Museum of American Art. Purchase, with funds from the Print Committee. 83.13

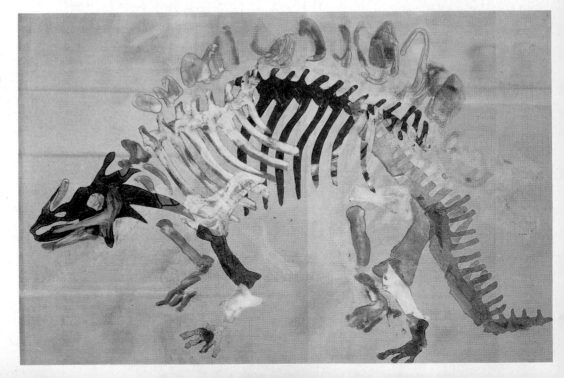

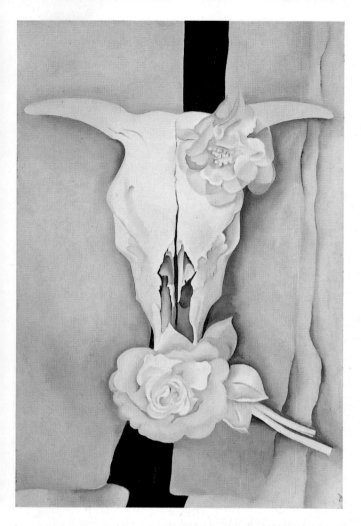

Cow's Skull with Calico Roses.
1932. Georgia O'Keeffe.

Oil on canvas, 91.2 x 61 cm. Gift of Georgia O'Keeffe,
The Art Institute of Chicago. 1947.712. © 1994 The Georgia O'Keeffe
Foundation/ARS, NY. Photo: © 1993 The Art Institute of Chicago.
All Rights Reserved

157

Desert Still Life. 1951.
Thomas Hart Benton.

Tempera with oil on linen mounted
on panel. Bequest of the artist, The
Nelson-Atkins Museum of Art,
Kansas City, Missouri. F75-21/45.
© 1993 Thomas Hart Benton and
Rita P. Benton Testamentary
Trusts/VAGA, NY

MONSTER TRACKS

Barbara Bruno

Snarl. Splash. Plop. Eek! Crunch. Just how did those bones and footprints come to be in these fossil rocks—rocks that tell a wordless story lost in time?

Sand-cast your own fossil clues from a past when monsters roamed and left odd tracks and dinner crumbs in the prehistoric ooze. First gather some feathers, twigs, bones (fish bones are fun), seashells, stones, or small sharp rocks to imprint or embed in sand.

Along with this interesting assortment of objects, you'll also need enough plaster of Paris to fill a mold, sand for shaping the mold, and a container. A plastic-lined, shallow cardboard box works well.

Wet the sand enough so that it keeps its shape when squeezed into a ball, then pack it into the box. Scoop out a flat area about an inch deep and as large as you want your fossil rock to be. Smooth the surface. You're ready to begin sand-casting.

To form the mold you must think in reverse. Holes poked in the sand will stick out. Sunken areas, like footprints, must be built up in the sand. Textures and other features can be made by pressing different objects into the sand. Seashells, bones, and other objects to be left in the sand casting must be pressed facedown into the sand. That way they'll rise above the finished casting's surface. (Half-buried things are interesting, too.)

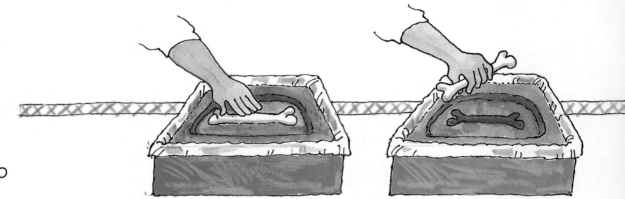

When you have finished making the mold, mix the plaster according to the instructions on the box. Mix only the amount you'll need to fill the mold. Slowly pour the plaster into the deepest parts of the mold first so that trapped air won't spoil the sand casting. Then carefully fill the rest of the mold.

When the sand casting has hardened completely (about fifteen minutes, depending on its size and thickness), carefully dig it up. Gently brush away as much of the sand as you can. Some sand will remain embedded in the plaster.

Your sand casting most likely won't look exactly as you expected, but the results are always fun to see. You can "age" your fossil rock by painting it with watercolors or rubbing mud into the deepest imprints.

BIBLIOGRAPHY

Dinosaur Hunters by Kate McMullan. How do scientists find out what prehistoric animals were like? Read this book about the work scientists do to learn about prehistoric creatures.

Dinosaurs, poems selected by Lee Bennett Hopkins. Let your imagination soar as you have fun with these wonderful poems about the mighty dinosaurs who once roamed the earth.

Dinosaur Story by Joanna Cole. From the study of their bones, learn what dinosaurs must have been like.

Fossils by Neil Curtis. What are fossils and how are they formed? This book answers these and other questions about fossils and prehistoric life.

Hunting the Dinosaurs and Other Prehistoric Animals by Dougal Dixon. This book lets you examine how paleontologists discover, study, classify, reconstruct, and restore the fossil remains of many kinds of dinosaurs.

If You Are a Hunter of Fossils by Byrd Baylor. Walk with a fossil hunter looking for signs of an ancient sea in the rocks of a western Texas mountain. This book takes an imaginative look at how the area must have appeared long ago.

In the Time of the Dinosaurs by William Wise. This book tells about dinosaurs that are long gone from our earth. Find out what the bones they left behind tell us about their world.

New Questions and Answers About Dinosaurs by Seymour Simon. Which dinosaur had the most teeth? How smart were dinosaurs? What colors were they? The answers to these questions and many more are in this book.

164

KINDNESS

165

THE ELVES AND THE SHOEMAKER

retold by *Freya Littledale*
illustrated by *Brinton Turkle*

There was once a good shoemaker who became
very poor. At last he had only one piece of
leather to make one pair of shoes.

"Well," said the shoemaker to his wife, "I will cut the
leather tonight and make the shoes in the morning."

The next morning he went to his table, and he
couldn't believe what he saw. The leather was polished.
The sewing was done. And there was a fine pair of shoes!
Not one stitch was out of place.

"Do you see what I see?" asked the shoemaker.

"Indeed I do," said his wife. "I see a fine pair of shoes."

"But who could have made them?" the shoemaker said.

"It's just like magic!" said his wife.

At that very moment a man came in with a top hat and cane. "Those shoes look right for me," said the man. And so they were. They were right from heel to toe. "How much do they cost?"

"One gold coin," said the shoemaker.

"I'll give you two," said the man.

And he went on his way with a smile on his face and the new shoes on his feet.

"Well, well," said the shoemaker, "now I can buy leather for two pairs of shoes." And he cut the leather that night so he could make the shoes in the morning.

The next morning the shoemaker woke up, and he found two pairs of ladies' shoes. They were shining in the sunlight.

"Who is making these shoes?" said the shoemaker. "They are the best shoes in the world."

At that very moment two ladies came in. They looked exactly alike. "My, what pretty shoes!" said the ladies. "They will surely fit us." And the ladies were right. They gave the shoemaker four gold coins and away they went . . . clickety-clack, clickety-clack in their pretty new shoes.

169

And so it went. Every night the shoemaker cut the leather. Every morning the shoes were made. And every day more people came to buy his beautiful shoes.

Just before Christmas the shoemaker said, "Whoever is making these shoes is making us very happy."

"And rich," said his wife.

"Let us stay up and see who it is," the shoemaker said.

"Good," said his wife. So they hid behind some coats, and they waited and waited and waited. When the clock struck twelve, in came two little elves. "*Elves,*" cried the shoemaker.

"Shh!" said his wife.

At once the elves hopped up on the table and set to work. Tap-tap went their hammers. Snip-snap went their scissors. Stitch-stitch went their needles. Their tiny fingers moved so fast the shoemaker and his wife could hardly believe their eyes.

The elves sewed and they hammered and they didn't stop until all the shoes were finished. There were little shoes and big ones. There were white ones and black ones and brown ones. The elves lined them all in a row. Then they jumped down from the table. They ran across the room and out the door.

171

The next morning the wife said, "The elves have made us very happy. I want to make them happy too. They need new clothes to keep warm. So I'll make them pants and shirts and coats. And I'll knit them socks and hats. You can make them each a pair of shoes."

"Yes, yes!" said the shoemaker. And they went right to work.

On Christmas Eve the shoemaker left no leather on the table. He left all the pretty gifts instead. Then he and his wife hid behind the coats to see what the elves would do.

When the clock struck twelve, in came the elves,
ready to set to work. But when they looked at the
table and saw the fine clothes, they laughed and
clapped their hands.

"How happy they are!" said the
shoemaker's wife.

"Shhh," said her husband.

The elves put on the clothes, looked in the mirror, and began to sing:

> *What fine and handsome elves are we,*
> *No longer cobblers will we be.*
> *From now on we'll dance and play,*
> *Into the woods and far away.*

They hopped over the table and jumped over the chairs. They skipped all around the room, danced out the door, and were never seen again.

But from that night on everything always went well for the good shoemaker and his wife.

MEET FREYA LITTLEDALE, AUTHOR

Freya Littledale spent much of her free time as a child reading. She especially enjoyed fairy tales. When she was nine years old, she began writing her own stories and poems. She always loved writing for children. She kept sharing her stories for the rest of her life.

MUSHROOM IN THE RAIN

Mirra Ginsburg

illustrated by Jose Aruego and Ariane Dewey

One day an ant was caught in the rain. "Where can I hide?" he wondered.

He saw a tiny mushroom peeking out of the ground in a clearing, and he hid under it. He sat there, waiting for the rain to stop. But the rain came down harder and harder.

A wet butterfly crawled up to the mushroom.

"Cousin Ant, let me come in from the rain. I am so wet I cannot fly."

"How can I let you in?" said the ant. "There is barely room enough for one."

"It does not matter," said the butterfly. "Better crowded than wet."

The ant moved over and made room for the butterfly. The rain came down harder and harder.

A mouse ran up.

"Let me in under the mushroom. I am drenched to the bone."

"How can we let you in? There is no more room here."

"Just move a little closer!"

They huddled closer and let the mouse in. And the rain came down and came down and would not stop.

A little sparrow hopped up to the mushroom, crying:
"My feathers are dripping, my wings are so tired! Let me
in under the mushroom to dry out and rest until the
rain stops!"

"But there is no room here."

"Please! Move over just a little!"

They moved over, and there was room enough for
the sparrow.

Then a rabbit hopped into the clearing and saw the mushroom.

"Oh, hide me!" he cried. "Save me! A fox is chasing me!"

"Poor rabbit," said the ant. "Let's crowd ourselves a little more and take him in."

As soon as they hid the rabbit, the fox came running.

"Have you seen the rabbit? Which way did he go?"
he asked.

"We have not seen him."

The fox came nearer and sniffed. "There is a rabbit
smell around. Isn't he hiding here?"

"You silly fox! How could a rabbit get in here? Don't you see there isn't any room?"

The fox turned up his nose, flicked his tail, and ran off.

By then the rain was over. The sun looked out from behind the clouds. And everyone came out from under the mushroom, bright and merry.

The ant looked at his neighbors. "How could this be?
At first I had hardly room enough under the mushroom
just for myself, and in the end all five of us were able to
sit under it."

"Qua-ha-ha! Qua-ha-ha!" somebody laughed loudly
behind them.

They turned and saw a fat green frog sitting on top of
the mushroom, shaking his head at them.

"Qua-ha-ha!" said
the frog. "Don't you
know what happens to
a mushroom in the
rain?" And he hopped
away, still laughing.

The ant, the butterfly, the mouse, the sparrow, and the rabbit looked at one another, then at the mushroom. And suddenly they knew why there was room enough under the mushroom for them all.

Do you know? Can you guess what happens to a mushroom when it rains?

IT GROWS!

185 Ⓒ

MEET MIRRA GINSBURG, AUTHOR

Mirra Ginsburg was born in a small Russian village much like the towns in the folk tales that she loved to read. She went to schools in other countries and finally in the United States. She learned English by reading poetry with the help of a dictionary.

Mirra Ginsburg began writing children's books by taking books written in Russian or Yiddish and rewriting them in English so that American children could enjoy them. Before long, she was making up her own stories. She says, "From my father, I learned to love animals and green growing things. As a child, I was surrounded with them."

THE CAMEL'S NOSE

retold by Franco Cour

illustrated by Kirsti Frigell

One cold night a man was sitting inside his tent. Suddenly the man's camel stuck its nose under the flap of the tent and said, "Master, be good enough to let me put my head inside the tent, for it is cold outside."

"Very well," said the man, "you may put your head inside my tent."

So the camel put its head into the tent. Then in a little while the camel said, "Good master, pray let me put my neck into the tent also. I may catch a chill if my head is warm and my neck is cold."

"Very well," replied the man, "you may put your neck into the tent, too."

After a little while the camel said again, "Kind master, allow me to put my forelegs into the tent. They take up only a little room, and it is uncomfortable standing this way."

"Very well," said the man, "you may do so." The man moved over to make room for the camel, for the tent was very small.

Then in a little while more the camel said, "Generous master, permit me to stand all the way inside the tent. I keep the flap of the tent open standing this way, and the cold air rushes inside."

"Very well, then," said the man. "You may come all the way inside."

The camel crowded its way into the tent, but the tent was too small for both man and camel.

"I think that there is not room for both of us in the tent," said the camel. "Since you are smaller than I, it would be better if you stood outside."

With these words the camel gave its master a little push.

Soon the man found himself standing outside
in the cold, while the camel was enjoying the warmth of
the tent.

As the man stood shivering from the cold, he said to
himself, "I can see now that it is better to stop bad
things before they get started."

CORDUROY
Don Freeman

Corduroy is a bear who once lived in the toy department of a big store. Day after day he waited with all the other animals and dolls for someone to come along and take him home.

The store was always filled with shoppers buying all sorts of things, but no one ever seemed to want a small bear in green overalls.

Then one morning a little girl stopped and looked straight into Corduroy's bright eyes.

"Oh, Mommy!" she said. "Look! There's the very bear I've always wanted."

"Not today, dear." Her mother sighed. "I've spent too much already. Besides, he doesn't look new. He's lost the button to one of his shoulder straps."

Corduroy watched them sadly as they walked away.

"I didn't know I'd lost a button," he said to himself. "Tonight I'll go and see if I can find it."

Late that evening, when all the shoppers had gone and the doors were shut and locked, Corduroy climbed carefully down from his shelf and began searching everywhere on the floor for his lost button.

Suddenly he felt the floor moving under him! Quite by accident he had stepped onto an escalator—and up he went!

"Could this be a mountain?" he wondered. "I think I've always wanted to climb a mountain."

He stepped off the escalator as it reached the next floor, and there, before his eyes, was a most amazing sight—tables and chairs and lamps and sofas, and rows and rows of beds. "This must be a palace!" Corduroy gasped. "I guess I've always wanted to live in a palace."

He wandered around admiring the furniture.

"This must be a bed," he said. "I've always wanted to sleep in a bed." And up he crawled onto a large, thick mattress.

All at once he saw something small and round.

"Why, here's my button!" he cried. And he tried to pick it up. But, like all the other buttons on the mattress, it was tied down tight.

He yanked and pulled with both paws until POP! Off came the button—and off the mattress Corduroy toppled, *bang* into a tall floor lamp. Over it fell with a crash!

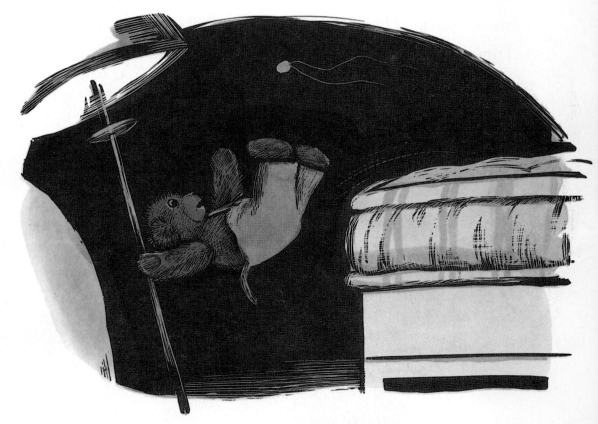

Corduroy didn't know it, but there was someone else awake in the store. The night watchman was going his rounds on the floor above. When he heard the crash he came dashing down the escalator.

"Now who in the world did that!" he exclaimed. "Somebody must be hiding around here!"

He flashed his light under and over sofas and beds until he came to the biggest bed of all. And there he saw two fuzzy brown ears sticking up from under the cover.

"Hello!" he said. "How did *you* get upstairs?"

195

The watchman tucked Corduroy under his arm and carried him down the escalator and set him on the shelf in the toy department with the other animals and dolls.

Corduroy was just waking up when the first customers came into the store in the morning. And there, looking at him with a wide, warm smile, was the same little girl he'd seen only the day before.

"I'm Lisa," she said, "and you're going to be my very own bear. Last night I counted what I've saved in my piggy bank and my mother said I could bring you home."

"Shall I put him in a box for you?" the saleslady asked.

"Oh, no thank you," Lisa answered. And she carried Corduroy home in her arms.

She ran all the way up four flights of stairs, into her family's apartment, and straight to her own room.

Corduroy blinked. There was a chair and a chest of drawers, and alongside a girl-size bed stood a little bed just the right size for him. The room was small, nothing like that enormous palace in the department store.

"This must be home," he said. "I *know* I've always wanted a home!"

Lisa sat down with Corduroy on her lap and began to sew a button on his overalls.

"I like you the way you are," she said, "but you'll be more comfortable with your shoulder strap fastened."

"You must be a friend," said Corduroy. "I've always wanted a friend."

"Me too!" said Lisa, and gave him a big hug.

MEET DON FREEMAN, AUTHOR AND ILLUSTRATOR

Don Freeman had a job playing the trumpet until one night he left his trumpet in the subway in New York City. He was so busy drawing for his art class that he forgot his trumpet. From then on, Freeman made his living drawing pictures. Freeman wrote and illustrated his first children's book for his young son, Roy. Many more books followed, including Corduroy.

CLARA BARTON:
RED CROSS PIONEER
Matthew G. Grant
illustrated by Charles Shaw

Clarissa Barton was 11 years old when her brother, David, fell off the barn. Doctors said David would probably die. But the little girl said, "I will take care of him."

For two years she tended him. In 1834, David finally got well. The doctor said, "Clara is a natural nurse. She has saved her brother's life."

Everyone called her Clara. She was the youngest in the family, a tiny girl who loved to ride horseback. She would listen wide-eyed to her father's tales of the Indian Wars. Sometimes she wept as he told how the wounded soldiers suffered.

Both her sisters and her eldest brother were teachers. When Clara was 18, she became a teacher, too. Her shyness melted away as she coped with rowdy boys. She became a great organizer, beloved for her sense of humor.

Clara taught school for 15 years. Several men wanted to marry her, but she told them she did not love them. She preferred to be independent.

In 1854, when she was 33, she was exhausted from teaching. She went to work as a clerk in the Patent Office in Washington—one of the first women to work in government. It was an interesting job and she made many friends among the politicians.

Then, in 1861, the Civil War broke out. Troops from Clara's home state of Massachusetts came to Washington—and they needed help.

The soldiers had been attacked by a mob. Their baggage had been stolen. Clara got her friends to provide clothes and other supplies for the men. She helped the soldiers write letters to their families.

Battles raged around Washington. Clara heard how wounded men were suffering on the battlefields and she determined to help them. First, she wrote to her friends, asking for money for medical supplies.

Clara Barton then went to Union Army officials and asked to be allowed to go to the battlefield in Virginia. Red tape was sliced freely to allow the determined little woman to carry out her plan.

Clara took a mule team loaded with medical supplies. She arrived at Culpeper, Virginia, two days after the Battle of Cedar Mountain. Wounded men lay everywhere. The army hospital was out of dressings. Clara and her supplies seemed like a miracle to the hard-working army doctors. She herself went to help the men still lying on the field. She fed them and gave them water. She brought warm clothes and comforted the dying.

Dr. James Dunn, the brigade surgeon, said, "She was like an angel. An angel of the battlefield."

Clara knew that the wounded would receive good care once they reached army hospitals. But her concern was for the men at the front. Many were dying of thirst and loss of blood before they could be safely evacuated. These were the men Clara set out to help. She did this work all through the war.

THE AMERICAN RED CROSS

When the Civil War ended, Clara Barton was famous. Almost single-handedly, she had changed the method of dealing with the wounded on the battlefield. She was treated as a heroine.

For some time, Clara devoted herself to the sad but necessary work of identifying unknown Union dead. She helped to set up a National Cemetery at Andersonville, Georgia, site of a large prison camp.

After this, Clara became a lecturer. She told eager listeners about her war work. She also became a champion of women's rights and a friend of Susan B. Anthony, Lucy Stone, and other pioneer feminists.

By 1869, Clara was once more very tired. She went on a vacation to Europe in order to regain her strength.

In Geneva, Switzerland, Dr. Louis Appia told her
about the work of the Red Cross. It was an international
group devoted to caring for the wounded in wartime.
Clara became keenly interested. At that time the
Franco-Prussian War broke out and Clara went to
observe the Red Cross in action.

Clara helped the suffering civilians of Strasbourg,
whose city had been pounded by a siege. She saw that
the Red Cross workers helped victims of war no matter
what their nationality. She resolved to do her best to
introduce the Red Cross into the United States.

But once more Clara's health broke down. It was several years before she returned home. Not until 1877 was she able to return to work.

When she was well again, she began urging Congress and the President to join the other nations of the world in the Red Cross. But at first she had no luck. People in government were sure that America would never again go to war. What need was there for the Red Cross? Clara pointed out that the Red Cross could be of service during natural disasters, too. She was the first to suggest this kind of Red Cross work.

In 1881, Clara set up the first local Red Cross unit in Dansville, New York. That very year there was a huge forest fire in Michigan. Red Cross units from Dansville, Rochester, and Syracuse sent help.

Newspapers wrote about the work of mercy. Other cities set up Red Cross units. Finally, on March 1, 1882, President Chester Arthur signed the Treaty of Geneva and the American Red Cross was born.

ONCE MORE INTO BATTLE

Clara Barton became the first president of the American Red Cross. She was an old woman but full of new energy. She helped organize Red Cross units all over the United States.

During the following years the Red Cross and Clara Barton aided the victims of floods, tornadoes, earthquakes, and disease epidemics. Red Cross workers not only nursed the sick and injured but also provided money to rebuild homes and replant lost crops.

The American Red Cross also helped to feed starving people in Russia and Armenia. In 1898, Clara took food to Cuba, where a revolution was raging.

The U.S. battleship Maine was blown up in Havana harbor. The Spanish-American War began. Once more Clara found herself aiding wounded Americans on the battlefield. She was 77 years old. When the war ended, Congress voted her the nation's thanks.

Clara Barton retired from the Red Cross in 1904. Not willing to be idle, she set up the National First Aid Association.

The rest of her days were spent in writing books about the Red Cross and her childhood, and letters to her many friends around the world. She still made an occasional speech and also found time to garden, repair furniture, and learn to typewrite.

Clara Barton died April 12, 1912, at the age of 91. She was buried at her birthplace, North Oxford, Massachusetts. The Red Cross flag is her monument.

210

The Good Samaritan. c. 1618–1622. Domenico Fetti.

Oil on panel. Rogers Fund, 1930, The Metropolitan Museum of Art. 30.31.
Photo: © 1979 The Metropolitan Museum of Art

General and horse. 7th century.
Stone relief from the tomb of
Emperor Tang Taizong.

University Museum,
University of Pennsylvania. C395

211 ②

Men Exist for the Sake of One Another.
Teach Them Then or Bear with Them.
1958. Jacob Lawrence.

THE NORTH WIND AND THE SUN

Aesop
retold by Margaret Clark
illustrated by Charlotte Voake

The north wind and the sun were having an argument. The north wind claimed to be stronger than the sun, and the sun said, "No, I am the strongest." At last they agreed to have a competition to see who could make a traveler take off his cloak.

The wind blew and blew furiously, but the harder it gusted the tighter the man clutched his cloak around him.

Then it was the sun's turn.
At first the sun warmed the traveler
gently with its rays so that he soon had
to unbutton his cloak. Then the sun
shone more and more brightly, until the
man was so hot that he threw off his
cloak and went on his way without it.

MUSIC, MUSIC FOR EVERYONE

Vera B. Williams

Our big chair sits in our living room empty now. When I first got my accordion, Grandma and Mama used to sit in that chair together to listen to me practice. And every day after school while Mama was at her job at the diner, Grandma would be sitting in the chair by the window. Even if it was snowing big flakes down on her hair, she would lean way out to call, "Hurry up, Pussycat. I've got something nice for you."

But now Grandma is sick. She has to stay upstairs in the big bed in Aunt Ida and Uncle Sandy's extra room. Mama and Aunt Ida and Uncle Sandy and I take turns taking care of her. When I come home from school, I run right upstairs to ask Grandma if she wants anything. I carry up the soup Mama has left for her. I water her plants and report if the Christmas cactus has any flowers yet. Then I sit on her bed and tell her about everything.

Grandma likes it when my friends Leora, Jenny, and Mae come home with me because we play music for her. Leora plays the drums. Mae plays the flute. Jenny plays fiddle and I play my accordion. One time we played a dance for Grandma that we learned in the music club at school.

Grandma clapped until it made her too tired.

215 ②

She told us it was like the music in the village where she lived when she was a girl. It made her want to dance right down the street. We had to keep her from trying to hop out of bed to go to the kitchen to fix us a treat.

Leora and Jenny and Mae and I left Grandma to rest and went down to get our own treat. We squeezed together into our big chair to eat it.

"It feels sad down here without your Grandma," Leora said. "Even your big money jar up there looks sad and empty."

"Remember how it was full to the top and I couldn't even lift it when we bought the chair for my mother?" I said.

"And remember how it was more than half full when you got your accordion?" Jenny said.

"I bet it's empty now because your mother has to spend all her money to take care of your grandma till she gets better. That's how it was when my father had his accident and couldn't go to work for a long time," Mae said.

Mae had a dime in her pocket and she dropped it into the jar. "That will make it look a little fuller anyway," she said as she went home.

But after Jenny and Leora and Mae went home, our jar looked even emptier to me. I wondered how we would ever be able to fill it up again while Grandma was sick. I wondered when Grandma would be able to come downstairs again. Even our beautiful chair with roses all over it seemed empty with just me in the corner of it. The whole house seemed so empty and so quiet.

I got out my accordion and I started to play. The notes sounded beautiful in the empty room. One song that is an old tune sounded so pretty I played it over and over. I remembered what my mother had told me about my other grandma and how she used to play the accordion.

Even when she was a girl not much bigger than I, she would get up and play at a party or a wedding so the company could dance and sing. Then people would stamp their feet and yell, "More, more!" When they went home, they would leave money on the table for her.

That's how I got my idea for how I could help fill up the jar again. I ran upstairs. "Grandma," I whispered. "Grandma?"

"Is that you, Pussycat?" she answered in a sleepy voice. "I was just having such a nice dream about you. Then I woke up and heard you playing that beautiful old song. Come. Sit here and brush my hair."

I brushed Grandma's hair and told her my whole idea. She thought it was a great idea. "But tell the truth, Grandma," I begged her. "Do you think kids could really do that?"

"I think you and Jenny and Leora and Mae could do it. No question. No question at all," she answered. "Only don't wait a minute to talk to them about it. Go call and ask them now."

And that was how the Oak Street Band got started.

Our music teachers helped us pick out pieces we could all play together. Aunt Ida, who plays guitar, helped us practice. We practiced on our back porch.

One day our neighbor leaned out his window in his pajamas and yelled, "Listen, kids, you sound great but give me a break. I work at night. I've got to get some sleep in the daytime." After that we practiced inside. Grandma said it was helping her get better faster than anything.

At last my accordion teacher said we sounded very good. Uncle Sandy said so too. Aunt Ida and Grandma said we were terrific. Mama said she thought anyone would be glad to have us play for them.

It was Leora's mother who gave us our first job.

She asked us to come and play at a party for Leora's great-grandmother and great-grandfather. It was going to be a special anniversary for them. It was fifty years ago on that day they first opened their market on our corner. Now Leora's mother takes care of the market. She always plays the radio loud while she works. But for the party she said there just had to be live music.

All of Leora's aunts and uncles and cousins came to the party. Lots of people from our block came too. Mama and Aunt Ida and Uncle Sandy walked down from our house very slowly with Grandma. It was Grandma's first day out.

There was a long table in the backyard made from little tables all pushed together. It was covered with so many big dishes of food you could hardly see the tablecloth. But I was too excited to eat anything.

Leora and Jenny and Mae and I waited over by the rosebush. Each of us had her instrument all ready. But everyone else went on eating and talking and eating some more. We didn't see how they would ever get around to listening to us. And we didn't see how we could be brave enough to begin.

At last Leora's mother pulled us right up in front of everybody. She banged on a pitcher with a spoon to get attention.

Then she introduced each one of us. "And now we're going to have music," she said. "Music and dancing for everyone."

It was quiet as school assembly. Every single person there was looking right at Leora and Jenny and Mae and me. But we just stood there and stared right back. Then I heard my grandma whisper, "Play, Pussycat. Play anything. Just like you used to play for me."

I put my fingers on the keys and buttons of my accordion. Jenny tucked her fiddle under her chin. Mae put her flute to her mouth. Leora held up her drums. After that we played and played. We made mistakes, but we played like a real band. The little lanterns came on. Everyone danced.

Mama and Aunt Ida and Uncle Sandy smiled at us every time they danced by. Grandma kept time nodding her head and tapping with the cane she uses now. Leora and Jenny and Mae and I forgot about being scared. We loved the sound of the Oak Street Band.

And afterward everybody clapped and shouted. Leora's great-grandfather and great-grandmother thanked us. They said we had made their party something they would always remember. Leora's father piled up plates of food for us. My mama arranged for Leora, Jenny, and Mae to stay over at our house. And when we finally all went out the gate together, late at night, Leora's mother tucked an envelope with our money into Leora's pocket.

As soon as we got home, we piled into my bed to divide the money. We made four equal shares. Leora said she was going to save up for a bigger drum. Mae wasn't sure what she would do with her share. Jenny fell asleep before she could tell us. But I couldn't even lie down until I climbed up and put mine right into our big jar on the shelf near our chair.

MEET VERA B. WILLIAMS, AUTHOR AND ILLUSTRATOR

When Vera Williams was nine years old, a painting of hers was exhibited in the Museum of Modern Art in New York City. She wrote and illustrated her first children's book when she was in high school. Since then, she has written and illustrated many colorful books about kind and generous children.

When asked about the research she does for her pictures, Williams answered, "Once in a while I have a child pose for some detail. For Music, Music for Everyone, I rented an accordion, got a book on how to play it and tried my hand slightly."

BIBLIOGRAPHY

Amy's Goose by Efner Tudor Holmes. A young girl saves a goose from the clutches of a hungry fox. Will she be able to nurse the goose back to health?

A Fairy Went a-Marketing by Rose Fyleman. Have fun with the kind actions of a fairy told in verse.

I Know a Lady by Charlotte Zolotow. Meet one of the nicest ladies you would want to know in this wonderful story.

The King at the Door by Brock Cole. When a young boy's acts of kindness come to the attention of the king, the king finds a great way to repay him.

The Lady and the Spider by Faith McNulty. A little spider lives happily in a head of lettuce in a lady's garden. But one day the lettuce is in the lady's kitchen to be made into a salad. What will happen to the little spider?

Once There Were No Pandas by Margaret Greaves. Chien-min, a little girl, tries to save a bear cub from death. This kind act puts her in great danger.

The Weaving of a Dream retold by Marilee Heyer. An old widow works for three years to weave a wonderful shawl, but a gust of wind lifts the shawl into the sky. How does the widow get it back?

Wolf's Favor by Fulvio Testa. Read about a wolf's act of kindness and the adventures it leads to in the animal kingdom.

GLOSSARY

accordion (ə korˊ dē ən) *n.* A musical instrument held in both hands and played by squeezing it while pressing the keys.

accordion

admire (ad mīrˊ) *v.* To be pleased with.

aid (ād) *v.* To help.

amazing (ə māˊ zing) *adj.* Surprising; causing wonder.

amber (amˊ bər) *n.* A hard, yellow material made of sticky sap that has become hard and turned into a fossil.

ancient (ānˊ shənt) *adj.* Very old; in times long past.

anniversary (anˊ ə vûrˊ sə rē) *n.* The date of a celebration that takes place once a year.

appear (ə pērˊ) *v.* To come into sight.

Pronunciation Key: at; lāte; câre; fäther; set; mē; it; kīte; ox; rōse; ô in bought; coin; bŏŏk; tōō; form; out; up; tûrn; ə sound in about, chicken, pencil, cannon, circus; **ch**air; **hw** in **wh**ich; ri**ng**; **sh**op; **th**in; **th**ere; **zh** in treasure.

Arctic (ärk´ tik) *n.* The very cold area around the North Pole.

arrange (ə rānj´) *v.* To make a plan for.

assembly (ə sem´ blē) *n.* A gathering of people for a special purpose.

assistant (ə sis´ tənt) *n.* A helper; a person whose job is to help another person.

avalanche (av´ ə lanch´) *n.* A large amount of snow, ice, or stones falling rapidly down the side of a mountain.

ax (aks) *n.* A sharp-edged cutting tool.

baggage (bag´ ij) *n.* Luggage; all the belongings that a traveler takes on a journey.

ball (bôl) *n.* A large, fancy party at which people dance.

beloved (bi luv´ id) *adj.* Dear; much loved.

brigade (bri gād´) *n.* A military unit; an organized group of soldiers.

brilliant (bril´ yənt) *adj.* Bright; sparkling.

buckskin (buk´ skin´) *n.* A leather made from the skin of a deer.

burrow (bûr´ ō) *v.* To dig a tunnel in the earth.

camel (kam´ əl) *n.* A large desert animal that has a hump on its back.

canal (kə nal´) *n.* A waterway made by people.

cane (kān) *n.* A stick to help a person in walking.

cargo bay (kär´ gō bā´) *n.* A space or a room on an aircraft used to hold things carried on a trip.

cease (sēs) *v.* To stop.

cellar (sel´ ər) *n.* A room underground.

champion (cham´ pē ən) *n.* A person who defends people or ideas.

churn (chûrn) *v.* To make butter; to shake or mix rapidly.

cider (sī´ dər) *n.* A drink made from apples.

cinder (sin´ dər) *n.* A small bit of coal or wood that has been burned until it is black.

claim (klām) *v.* To say that something is true.

clearing (klēr´ ing) *n.* In a forest, a piece of land with no trees or bushes.

clearing

clerk (klûrk) *n.* An office worker.

climate (klī´ mit) *n.* The weather in an area.

cloak (klōk) *n.* A long, loose coat with no sleeves.

coachman (kōch´ mən) *n.* A person who drives a carriage.

coal (kōl) *n.* A hard, black material that is burned as fuel.

cobbler (kob´ lər) *n.* A person who makes and repairs shoes.

colossal (kə los´ əl) *adj.* Huge; very, very big.

Comanche (kə man´ chē) *n.* A Native American people of the Great Plains.

combined (kəm bīnd´) *adj.* Put together; mixed together.

comfort (kum´ fərt) *v.* To soothe; to cheer; to make someone feel better.

competition (kom´ pi tish´ ən) *n.* 1. The act of struggling to do better than another. 2. A contest to see who can do something better.

cope (kōp) *v.* To handle successfully; to deal with.

council (koun´ səl) *n.* An assembly or group that talks about problems and makes decisions.

court (kort) *n.* A king's or queen's palace.

crept (krept) *v.* A past tense of **creep:** To move silently on tiptoes or on hands and knees.

degree (di grē´) *n.* An award for graduating from college.

department (di pärt´ mənt) *n.* A single area of a store; a part of a store where one type of item is sold.

desert (dez´ ərt) *n.* A large land area with little or no water and sand instead of dirt.

determination (di tûr´ mə nā´ shən) *n.* A strength of purpose.

determine (di tûr´ min) *v.* To decide.

determined (di tûr´ mind) *adj.* Set; decided.

devote (di vōt´) *v.* To give full attention to.

229

Pronunciation Key: at; lāte; câre; fäther; set; mē; it; kīte; ox; rōse; ô in bought; coin; boŏk; tōō; form; out; up; tûrn; ə sound in about, chicken, pencil, cannon, circus; **ch**air; **hw** in **wh**ich; ri**ng**; **sh**op; **th**in; **th**ere; **zh** in trea**s**ure.

dike (dīk) *n.* A thick wall built to hold back water.

diner (dī′ nər) *n.* A small restaurant where the food does not cost very much money.

disappear (dis′ ə pēr′) *v.* 1. To leave someone's sight; to stop being seen. 2. To stop living.

disease (di zēz′) *n.* An illness; a sickness.

dissolve (di zolv′) *v.* To become part of a liquid; to melt.

distant (dis′ tənt) *adj.* A long time ago.

doctoral degree (dok′ tər əl di gree′) *n.* An award for graduating from the highest level at college.

dome (dōm) *n.* A rounded roof.

dome

drenched (drencht) *adj.* Wet all the way through; soaked.

dressing (dres′ ing) *n.* A bandage or other covering for a wound.

drought (drout) *n.* Dry weather for a long time; a long time with no rain.

earthquake (ûrth′ kwāk′) *n.* An underground shock that makes part of the earth's surface shake.

echo (ek′ ō) *n.* A sound that seems to be repeated because it is thrown back from far away.

educator (ej′ ŏŏ kā′ tər) *n.* A person who works in the schools, such as a teacher or a principal.

eject (i jekt′) *v.* To throw out.

elder (el′ dər) *n.* An older, important member of a tribe or family.

eldest (el′ dist) *adj.* Oldest.

elves (elvz) *n.* The plural of **elf:** A fairy who plays tricks.

embed (em bed′) *v.* To set something into a material.

engineer (en′ jə nēr′) *n.* A person who is in charge of operating a machine.

enormous (i nôr′ məs) *adj.* Huge; vast.

230

entry (en´ trē) *n.* The act of coming from outer space into the air around the earth.

epidemic (ep´ i dem´ ik) *n.* A disease that spreads quickly to many people.

erupt (i rupt´) *v.* To burst out; to explode.

escalator (es´ kə lā´ tər) *n.* A moving stairway.

evacuate (i vak´ yo͞o āt´) *v.* To leave an area; to make everyone leave.

exclaim (ik sklām´) *v.* To cry out suddenly.

exhausted (ig zôs´ tid) *adj.* Very tired; worn out.

experiment (ik sper´ ə mənt) *n.* A test; a trial; something done in order to find out what will happen.

famine (fam´ in) *n.* A great lack of food in an area or region.

famous (fā´ məs) *adj.* Well known; known by many people.

feast (fēst) *v.* To eat very well; to eat a lot of good food. —*n.* A large, fancy meal.

feebly (fē´ blē) *adv.* Weakly.

feminist (fem´ ə nist) *n.* A person who believes that women should have the same rights as men.

flap (flap) *n.* A hanging strip of some material.

flick (flik) *v.* To move in a rapid or jerky way.

flight deck (flīt´ dek´) *n.* A room in a spacecraft that holds the controls for flying.

flood (flud) *v.* To cover with water.

foreleg (for´ leg´) *n.* One of the front legs of an animal.

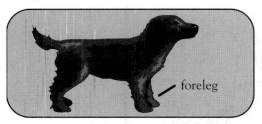
foreleg

231

forgave (fər gāv´) *v.* The past tense of forgive: To pardon; to excuse.

front (frunt) *n.* The place where fighting takes place in a war.

gasp (gasp) *v.* To breathe in gulps with the mouth wide open.

generous (jen´ ər əs) *adj.* Not selfish; freely giving or sharing.

Pronunciation Key: at; lāte; câre; fäther; set; mē; it; kīte; ox; rōse; ô in bought; coin; bŏŏk; tōō; form; out; up; tûrn; ə sound in about, chicken, pencil, cannon, circus; chair; hw in which; ring; shop; thin; then; zh in treasure.

government (guv´ ərn mənt) *n.* All the people who work to rule a country.

gown (goun) *n.* A woman's dress, often fancy.

grant (grant) *v.* To give; to allow.

greedy (grē´ dē) *adj.* Always wanting more.

gurgling (gûr´ gling) *adj.* Making a noise like bubbling water.

gust (gust) *v.* To blow in short bursts.

guts (guts) *n. slang.* Courage; bravery.

hauling (hôl´ ing) *n.* Pulling.

hayfield (hā´ fēld´) *n.* The land where a farmer grows grass to make hay.

healing (hēl´ ing) *adj.* Making healthy; curing.

hero (hēr´ ō) *n.* A person who does brave or important things to help others.

heroine (her´ ō in) *n.* A woman who does brave or important things to help others.

homesick (hōm´ sik´) *adj.* Sad due to wanting to go home; missing one's home.

huddle (hud´ l) *v.* To crowd together.

identify (ī den´ tə fī´) *v.* To recognize; to know; to be able to name.

idle (īd´ l) *adj.* 1. Useless; lazy. 2. Not busy; not working at anything.

Iguanodon (i gwä´ nə don´) *n.* A dinosaur that walked on two feet and ate only plants.

impatient (im pā´ shənt) *adj.* Annoyed at delay; not happy to be kept waiting.

imprint (im´ print) *n.* A mark made by pressing. —*v.* (im print´) To make a mark by pressing.

independent (in´ di pen´ dənt) *adj.* Free; thinking and acting for oneself; not controlled by others.

influence (in´ flōō əns) *n.* The ability to make people think a certain way.

inn (in) *n.* A hotel; a building where people pay to stay overnight.

innkeeper (in´ kē´ pər) *n.* A person who owns or runs an inn or a hotel.

international (in´ tər nash´ ə nl) *adj.* Having to do with all nations or countries.

introduce (in´ trə dōōs´) *v.* To have people meet each other for the first time; to tell someone who someone else is.

issue (ish´ ōō) *v.* To publish; to send out.

jug (jug) *n.* A deep container with a handle, used for holding things to drink.

knead (nēd) *v.* To work dough by pressing, folding, and squeezing.

lack (lak) *n.* A need; a shortage; not enough of something.

lantern (lan´ tərn) *n.* A box with a light inside that can be seen shining on the outside.

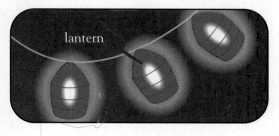

lantern

launching (lônch´ ing) *n.* Sending a spaceship out into space; the start of a space trip.

launchpad (lônch´ pad´) *n.* A raised floor or platform on which a spacecraft stands when it is being sent out into space.

leather (leth´ ər) *n.* The skin of an animal after it has been tanned, or softened; for use in making shoes and other items.

lecturer (lek´ chər ər) *n.* A person who gives speeches to teach a class or group.

long (lông) *v.* To desire; to want.

mammoth (mam´ əth) *n.* A large, hairy elephant that lived millions of years ago.

market (mär´ kit) *n.* A place in which things are bought and sold; a store.

master's degree (mas´ tərz di grē´) *n.* An award for completing more college work than a four-year program.

mercy (mûr´ sē) *n.* Kind feelings.

method (meth´ əd) *n.* A way of doing things.

233

Pronunciation Key: at; lāte; câre; fäther; set; mē; it; kīte; ox; rōse; ô in bought; coin; bŏŏk; tōō; form; out; up; tûrn; ə sound in about, chicken, pencil, cannon, circus; chair; hw in which; ring; shop; thin; there; zh in treasure.

mineral (min´ ər əl) *n.* A natural substance from the earth that is not an animal or a plant.

miraculous (mi rak´ yə ləs) *adj.* Like a miracle; marvelous.

mission (mish´ ən) *n.* All the planning and the people who carry out a space flight.

mission specialist (mish´ ən spesh´ ə list) *n.* A person who is on the crew of a spaceship.

monument (mon´ yə mənt) *n.* Something made in memory of a person; something that makes people think of a certain person.

monumental (mon´ yə men´ tl) *adj.* Large and important.

mural (myŏŏr´ əl) *n.* A picture painted on a wall.

museum (myōō zē´ əm) *n.* A building where people can look at works of art or interesting objects from history or nature.

234

nationality (nash´ ə nal´ i tē) *n.* A person's membership in a particular nation.

natural disaster (nach´ ər əl di zas´ tər) *n.* Great damage caused by an event of nature such as a storm, a flood, or an earthquake.

notice (nō´ tis) *v.* To see.

numb (num) *adj.* Having no feeling; not able to feel anything in some part of the body.

observe (əb zûrv´) *v.* To watch.

official (ə fish´ əl) *n.* A person who has public duties; a person who is elected to work for the government.

ooze (ōōz) *n.* Slush; slime; watery mud.

orbit (or´ bit) *n.* The circle-shaped path of the earth, moon, or any planet or heavy body. —*v.* To travel in a circle around something else.

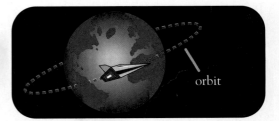

orbit

organizer (or´ gə nī´ zər) *n.* A person who plans or arranges things.

overalls (ō´ vər ôlz´) *n.* Loose trousers with a bib front and straps at the shoulders.

page (pāj) *n.* A boy servant.

palace (pal´ is) *n.* A large, fancy house; the home of a king and queen.

pastor (pas´ tər) *n.* The minister of a church.

patent (pat´ nt) *n.* The right of an inventor to make others pay for using the invention.

patient (pā´ shənt) *adj.* Calm; willing to wait; not complaining.

pen name (pen´ nām´) *n.* A name that a writer makes up to use on books instead of his or her real name.

piece (pēs) *n.* An example of art or music; a composition.

pinky (ping´ kē) *n.* The little finger on a person's hand; the finger farthest from the thumb.

pioneer (pī´ ə nēr´) *n.* The first to explore something or try to do something.

plentiful (plen´ ti fəl) *adj.* Having more than enough; abundant.

polish (pol´ ish) *v.* To make smooth and shiny by rubbing.

politician (pol´ i tish´ ən) *n.* A person who holds a public office or wants to be elected to a public office.

possession (pə zesh´ ən) *n.* Something that a person owns.

prefer (pri fûr´) *v.* To like better; to want to do one thing more than another.

prehistoric (prē´ hi stor´ ik) *adj.* Belonging to a time millions of years ago, before history was written down.

preserve (pri zûrv´) *v.* To save in good condition; to keep from rotting.

proclamation (prok´ lə mā´ shən) *n.* A public announcement; a statement to the people.

prodigious (prə dij´ əs) *adj.* Enormous; monstrous.

qualified (kwol´ ə fīd´) *adj.* Fit for something; having the skills needed for some task.

235

Pronunciation Key: at; lāte; câre; fäther; **set**; mē; **it**; kīte; ox; rōse; ô in bought; coin; boŏk; tōo; form; out; **up**; tûrn; ə sound in **a**bout, chick**e**n, penc**i**l, cann**o**n, circ**u**s; **ch**air; **hw** in **wh**ich; ri**ng**; **sh**op; **th**in; **th**ere; **zh** in trea**s**ure.

red tape (red′ tāp′) *n.* Papers and forms that must be filled out before government workers can take action.

reply (ri plī′) *v.* To answer.

resolve (ri zolv′) *v.* To decide.

restore (ri stor′) *v.* To give back; to return.

retire (ri tīr′) *v.* To leave employment; to stop working for a living.

reverse (ri vûrs′) *n.* The opposite way; backward.

revolution (rev′ ə lōo′ shən) *n.* A war in which people try to defeat the government of their own country.

robot arm (rō′ bət ärm′) *n.* A machine that can move and do things that a human arm can do.

rounds (roundz) *n.* The same trip taken over and over; a route taken that begins each time in the same place.

rowdy (rou′ dē) *adj.* Rough; acting like a bully.

rumble (rum′ bəl) *v.* To make a low, rolling sound like thunder.

sacrifice (sak′ rə fīs′) *v.* To give something up as an offering.

sap (sap) *n.* The juice from a plant.

satellite (sat′ l īt′) *n.* Any heavy body that travels in a circle around another object.

scientist (sī′ ən tist) *n.* A person who studies nature and natural laws.

scroll (skrōl) *n.* A roll of paper used for writing, especially many years ago.

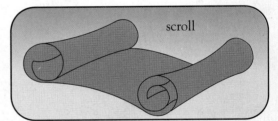

scroll

seep (sēp) *v.* To leak out drop by drop; to ooze.

Seismosaurus (sīs′ mə sor′ əs) *n.* A dinosaur that was about 110 feet long and 50 feet tall.

sexton (sek′ stən) *n.* A person who takes care of a church building.

shallow (shal′ ō) *adj.* Not deep.

shaman (shä´ mən) *n.* The person who acts as a connection between a tribe and the forces of nature; the person who leads a tribe in spiritual matters.

shiver (shiv´ ər) *v.* To tremble or shake from the cold or from fear.

shoemaker (shoo´ mā´ kər) *n.* A person who makes or repairs shoes.

shopper (shop´ ər) *n.* A person who is looking for things to buy.

siege (sēj) *n.* An attack that takes a very long time.

sigh (sī) *v.* To let out a loud breath.

simpleton (sim´ pəl tən) *n.* A person who does not know very much.

simulation (sim´ yə lā´ shən) *n.* The act of pretending.

single-handedly (sing´ gəl han´ did lē) *adv.* Done by one person alone.

site (sīt) *n.* The place where a building or city is located.

sniff (snif) *v.* To smell; to draw a short breath up the nose.

so (sō) *adj.* True.

sofa (sō´ fə) *n.* A couch with a back and two arms.

solid (sol´ id) *adj.* Completely filled, with no empty spaces inside.

soot (soot) *n.* Tiny black bits of something that has burned, such as wood or coal.

sought (sôt) *v.* A past tense of **seek:** To look for; to try to find.

spirit (spir´ it) *n.* A being without a body.

sprinkler (spring´ klər) *n.* A device that scatters drops of water.

stupendous (stoo pen´ dəs) *adj.* Amazingly large.

succeed (sək sēd´) *v.* To take someone's job after that person quits; to follow in a job after someone else.

successor (sək ses´ ər) *n.* A person who takes over another person's job.

superintendent (soo´ pər in ten´ dənt) *n.* The person in charge of a place.

supplies (sə plīz´) *n.* The things needed for a certain task or purpose.

surgeon (sûr´ jən) *n.* A doctor who operates on people to make them well.

swamp (swomp) *n.* An area of low, wet ground; a marsh.

swampy (swom´ pē) *adj.* Soft and wet.

237

Pronunciation Key: at; lāte; câre; fäther; set; mē; it; kīte; ox; rōse; ô in bought; coin; bŏŏk; tōō; form; out; up; tûrn; ə sound in about, chicken, pencil, cannon, circus; chair; hw in which; ring; shop; thin; there; zh in treasure.

swat (swot) *v.* To hit with a quick, hard blow.

swirl (swûrl) *v.* To spin around; to turn around rapidly.

swung (swung) *v.* A past tense of **swing:** To move something back and forth.

tend (tend) *v.* To take care of; to care for.

thrust (thrust) *v.* To push into with force.

tipi (tē´ pē) *n.* A tent of some Native Americans. Also spelled *tepee.*

titanic (tī tan´ ik) *adj.* Great in size or power.

tool (tōōl) *n.* An instrument used to do work, often held in the hands.

top hat (top´ hat´) *n.* A man's hat that has a tall top shaped like a tube.

topple (top´ əl) *v.* To fall down.

transfer (trans fûr´) *v.* To move something from one place to another.

tremble (trem´ bəl) *v.* To shake; to shiver.

tremendous (tri men´ dəs) *adj.* Enormous; huge.

trickle (trik´ əl) *v.* To flow in a small stream.

troops (trōōps) *n.* A group of soldiers.

tropical (trop´ i kəl) *adj.* Very hot and humid; in the part of the earth near the equator.

uncomfortable (un kumf´ tə bəl) *adj.* Not at ease; feeling disturbed or in pain.

unit (yōō´ nit) *n.* One part of a larger organization.

unknown (un nōn´) *adj.* 1. Not well known; not known by name. 2. Not discovered; not explored.

urge (ûrj) *v.* To try to talk someone into doing something.

village (vil´ ij) *n.* A small group of houses in the country; a country settlement that is smaller than a town.

238

volcano (vol kā´ nō) *n.* A hole in the earth that throws out smoke, melted rock, and ashes, forming a mountain.

volcano

wand (wond) *n.* A magic rod; a stick that is used for magic.

warmth (wôrmth) *n.* Heat.

wartime (wor´ tīm´) *n.* The period of time when nations are fighting.

watchman (woch´ mən) *n.* A man whose job is to guard property.

water bug (wô´ tər bug´) *n.* A very large, slow-moving insect.

wept (wept) *v.* A past tense of **weep:** To cry; to sob; to shed tears.

will (wil) *n.* A person's purpose; the strong feeling of being able to do something.

wimp (wimp) *n. slang.* A person who is weak and afraid.

windmill (wind´ mil´) *n.* A tall structure with sails on poles, or "arms," that stick out from the top and spin around using the power of the wind. When the arms spin, a machine inside grinds up grain or pumps water.

windmill

wisdom (wiz´ dəm) *n.* The ability to decide what is true or right; the state of being wise.

wisest (wīz´ əst) *adj.* Most intelligent; smartest.

woodcutter (wŏŏd´ kut´ ər) *n.* A person who cuts down trees to sell the wood.

wordless (wûrd´ lis) *adj.* Silent.

wounded (wōōn´ did) *adj.* Injured; hurt.

yon (yon) *adv.* Yonder; over there.

239

COLOPHON

*This book has been designed in the classic
style to emphasize our commitment to classic
literature. The typeface, Goudy Old Style, was
drawn in 1915 by Frederic W. Goudy, who based it
on fifteenth-century Italian letterforms.*

*The art has been drawn to reflect the golden age
of children's book illustration and its recent rebirth
in the work of innovative artists of today.
This book was designed by John Grandits.
Composition, electronic page makeup, and photo
and art management were provided by
The Chestnut House Group, Inc.*